100
Best
Stir-Fries

100
Best
Stir-Fries

The ultimate guide to great stir-fries including
100 delicious recipes

First published in 2012
LOVE FOOD is an imprint of Parragon Books Ltd

Parragon
Queen Street House
4 Queen Street
Bath BA1 1HE, UK

www.parragon.com

ISBN: 978-1-4454-6196-0

Printed in Indonesia

Introduction by Linda Doeser

Notes for the Reader
This book uses standard kitchen measuring spoons and cups. All spoon
and cup measurements are level unless otherwise indicated. Unless
otherwise stated, milk is assumed to be whole, eggs are large, individual
vegetables are medium, and pepper is freshly ground black pepper.

The times given are only an approximate guide. Preparation times differ
according to the techniques used by different people and the cooking
times may also vary from those given. Optional ingredients, variations, or
serving suggestions have not been included in the calculations.

Recipes using raw or very lightly cooked eggs should be avoided by
infants, the elderly, pregnant women, and anyone with a chronic illness.
Pregnant and breast-feeding women are advised to avoid eating peanuts
and peanut products. People with nut allergies should be aware that
some of the prepared ingredients used in the recipes in this book may
contain nuts. Always check the packaging before use.

Picture acknowledgments
The publishers would like to thank Getty Images/Juptiterimages for
permission to reproduce copyright material on the front cover.

CONTENTS

INTRODUCTION

It might have been invented centuries ago in China, but stir-frying is the perfect technique for today's busy Western cook. A huge array of sensational dishes can be prepared and cooked quickly and easily, whether for midweek family dinners or informal entertaining.

The secret of stir-frying is simple. Ingredients are finely chopped or thinly sliced so that they are all about the same size and then added to a hot wok containing a little oil. Aromatics, such as garlic and scallions, are added first, then the ingredients that require longer cooking, such as meat and denser vegetables, and, finally, the quick-cooking items, such as green vegetables and noodles. The contents of the wok are stirred and tossed throughout the cooking time. This ensures that they are cooked through rapidly without losing their color, texture, or nutrients.

Although you can make a stir-fry in a skillet, using a wok is far easier and more effective. A wok is a deep pan with sloping sides, designed for the continuous movement of the contents as they are tossed and return to the center, where the heat is the most intense. The best woks are made of carbon steel or cast iron; stainless steel tends to scorch. A wok with a round bottom works well on a gas stove top, and one with a slightly flattened bottom is suitable for electric or ceramic stove tops. A good size for cooking a family meal is a wok with a diameter of 14 inches because it allows plenty of room for stirring without being awkward to handle.

Hints & tips
• Only tender cuts of meat and poultry and perfectly fresh vegetables are suitable for stir-frying because cooking takes a short amount of time.

• Prepare all the ingredients before you start to cook and make sure you have any flavorings, such as soy sauce, on hand. There will be no time for chopping or slicing once the first ingredients go into the wok.

• Use a sharp cook's knife or a Chinese cleaver for slicing and chopping. Slice denser vegetables, such as carrots and zucchini, diagonally. Exposing a large surface area to the heat ensures even and quick cooking.

• Always cut beef across the grain; lamb, pork, and chicken may be cut across or along the grain.

• Preheat the empty wok over high heat before adding the oil and swirling it to coat the bottom and halfway up the sides. You need far less oil than for ordinary pan-frying.

• Add the ingredients in the order specified in the recipe, and cook, stirring and tossing them from the center to the sides of the wok.

Seasoning the wok
Manufacturers protect steel and cast-iron woks with a coating to prevent rust. Heat the new wok, scrub in warm soapy water to remove the coating, then rinse and dry. The manufacturer's instructions will describe how to season the wok, usually by repeatedly rubbing with vegetable oil, heating, and then rubbing off the oil with paper towels. Once the wok has been seasoned, do not scrub again; simply wash in hot water.

1

APPETIZERS, SOUPS & SALADS

01

Egg Rolls

MAKES 20–25 PIECES

6 dried Chinese mushrooms, soaked
in warm water for 20 minutes

1 tablespoon peanut oil or vegetable
oil, plus extra for deep-frying

8 ounces fresh ground pork

1 teaspoon dark soy sauce

3/4 cup of drained and rinsed canned
bamboo shoots, julienned

4 ounces shrimp, peeled, deveined,
and chopped

2 1/2 cups coarsely chopped
bean sprouts

1 tablespoon scallions,
finely chopped

20–25 egg roll wrappers

1 egg white, lightly beaten

salt

Method

1 Squeeze out any excess water from the mushrooms and finely slice, discarding any tough stems.

2 In a preheated wok or deep skillet, heat the oil and stir-fry the pork until it changes color.

3 Add the dark soy sauce, bamboo shoots, and mushrooms, and season with a little salt. Stir over high heat for 3 minutes.

4 Add the shrimp and cook for 2 minutes, then add the bean sprouts and cook for another minute. Remove from the heat and stir in the scallions. Let cool.

5 Place a tablespoon of the mixture toward the bottom of a wrapper. Roll once to secure the filling, then fold in the sides to create a 4-inch piece and continue to roll up. Seal with egg white.

6 Heat enough oil for deep-frying in a wok, deep-fat fryer, or large, heavy saucepan until it reaches 350–375°F, or until a cube of bread browns in 30 seconds. Fry the rolls for about 5 minutes, until golden brown and crispy.

7 Transfer the egg rolls to serving bowls and serve.

02

Crispy Pork Dumplings

SERVES 4

3 scallions, coarsely chopped

1 garlic clove, coarsely chopped

1 small fresh red chile, seeded and
  coarsely chopped

8 ounces fresh ground pork

1 teaspoon salt

20 wonton wrappers

peanut oil or vegetable oil,
  for deep-frying

chiles, cut into flowers, to garnish

Method

1 Put the scallions, garlic, chile, pork, and salt in a food processor and process to a smooth paste.

2 Remove the wonton wrappers from the package, but keep them in a pile and cover with a clean, damp dish towel to prevent them from drying out. Lay one wrapper on a work surface in front of you in a diamond shape and brush the edges with water. Put a small amount of filling near one edge and fold the wrapper over the filling. Press the edges together to seal the bundle and shape into a semicircle. Repeat with the remaining wrappers and filling.

3 Heat the oil in a wok, deep saucepan, or deep-fat fryer to 350–375°F, or until a cube of bread browns in 30 seconds. Add the dumplings, in batches, and cook for 45 seconds–1 minute, until crisp and golden all over. Remove with a slotted spoon, drain on paper towels, and keep warm while you cook the remaining dumplings. Serve immediately, garnished with chile flowers.

03

Pork & Cabbage Gyoza

MAKES 24 PIECES

24 gyoza wonton skins

2 tablespoons water, for brushing

vegetable oil, for frying

2 tablespoons Japanese rice vinegar

2 tablespoons shoyu (Japanese soy sauce)

Filling

1 cup finely shredded cabbage

2 scallions, finely chopped

4 ounces fresh ground pork

1/2-inch piece fresh ginger, finely grated

2 garlic cloves, crushed

1 tablespoon shoyu (Japanese soy sauce)

2 teaspoons mirin

pinch of white pepper

salt, to taste

Method

1 To make the filling, mix all the ingredients together in a bowl.

2 Lay a gyoza wonton skin in the palm of your hand and place 1 heaping teaspoon of the filling in the center. Brush a little water around the edges of the wonton skin.

3 Fold the skin sides up to meet in a ridge along the center and press the edges together. Brush the curved edges of the skin with a little more water and make a series of little folds along the edges.

4 Repeat with the remaining gyoza wonton wrappers and filling. Heat a little oil in a wok or deep skillet with a lid and add as many gyoza as will fill the bottom of the wok with just a little space in between.

5 Cook for 2 minutes, or until browned. Add water to a depth of 1/8 inch, cover the wok, and let simmer over low heat for 6 minutes, or until the wrappers are translucent and cooked. Remove and keep warm while you cook the remaining gyoza.

6 Put the vinegar in a small dipping dish, stir in the shoyu, and add a splash of water.

7 Transfer the gyoza to a serving dish and serve with the sauce for dipping.

04

Chinese Rice with Egg

SERVES 2

2 teaspoons peanut oil
or vegetable oil

a few drops of sesame oil

1 small garlic clove, finely chopped

pinch of five-spice powder

1 carrot, diced

2 ears of baby corn, halved and
thinly sliced

2 tablespoons water

small handful of baby spinach,
trimmed and finely sliced

1¼ cups chilled cooked brown or
white rice

dash of soy sauce

1 teaspoon sesame seeds (optional)

small pat of butter

1 egg, beaten

Method

1 Heat a wok over medium–high heat, then add the oils. Add the garlic, five-spice powder, carrot, and baby ears of corn and stir-fry for 5 minutes, stirring and tossing continuously to prevent the spices and vegetables from burning and sticking.

2 Add the water and stir-fry for 2 minutes, then mix in the spinach and cook, stirring frequently, for another 2 minutes, or until the vegetables are tender.

3 Add the rice and soy sauce to the wok and heat through. Mix in the sesame seeds, if using.

4 Meanwhile, melt the butter in a small, heavy skillet and add the egg. Swirl the egg until it covers the botton of the skillet. Cook until the egg has set and is cooked through, then turn out onto a plate. Cut the omelet into strips or pieces.

5 Transfer the rice to individual serving bowls and arrange the omelet on top.

05

Shrimp Toasts

MAKES 16 PIECES

4 ounces shrimp, peeled
and deveined

2 egg whites

2 tablespoons cornstarch

1/2 teaspoon sugar

pinch of salt

2 tablespoons finely chopped fresh
cilantro leaves

2 slices day-old white bread

peanut oil or vegetable oil,
for deep-frying

Method

1 Pound the shrimp to a pulp with a pestle in a mortar.

2 Mix the shrimp with one of the egg whites and 1 tablespoon of the cornstarch. Add the sugar and salt and stir in the cilantro. Mix the remaining egg white with the remaining cornstarch.

3 Remove the crusts from the bread and cut each slice into 8 triangles. Brush the top of each piece with the egg white-and-cornstarch mixture, then add 1 teaspoon of the shrimp mixture. Smooth the top.

4 Heat enough oil for deep-frying in a wok, deep-fat fryer, or large, heavy saucepan until it reaches 350–375°F, or until a cube of bread browns in 30 seconds. Cook the toasts shrimp-side down for about 2 minutes. Turn and cook for another 2 minutes until golden.

5 Remove the shrimp toasts with a slotted spoon, drain on paper towels, and serve warm.

06

Crispy Sesame Shrimp

SERVES 4

1 cup self-rising flour

3 tablespoons sesame seeds,
  toasted or dry-fried

1 teaspoon Thai red curry paste

1 tablespoon Thai fish sauce

2/3 cup water

peanut oil or vegetable oil,
  for deep-frying

20 large, uncooked shrimp, peeled
  and deveined with tails intact

chili sauce, to serve

Method

1 Combine the flour and sesame seeds in a bowl. Stir together the curry paste, fish sauce, and water in a pitcher until mixed. Gradually pour the liquid into the flour, stirring continuously, to make a thick batter.

2 Heat a large wok over high heat. Pour in the oil and heat to 350–375°F, or until a cube of bread browns in 30 seconds. Holding the shrimp by their tails, dip them into the batter, one at a time, then carefully drop into the hot oil. Cook for 2–3 minutes, until crisp and brown. Drain on paper towels.

3 Serve immediately with chili sauce.

07

Crab Wontons

SERVES 4

1 tablespoon peanut oil or vegetable oil, plus extra for deep-frying

1-inch piece fresh ginger, peeled and finely chopped

1/4 red bell pepper, seeded and finely chopped

handful of fresh cilantro, chopped

1/4 teaspoon salt

5-ounce can white crabmeat, drained

20 wonton wrappers

water, for brushing

sweet chili dipping sauce, to serve

Method

1 Heat the oil in a preheated wok.

2 Add the ginger and red bell pepper and stir-fry over high heat for 30 seconds.

3 Add the cilantro and mix well. Let cool, then add the salt and crabmeat and mix well. Meanwhile, remove the wonton wrappers from the package, but keep them in a pile and cover with a clean, damp dish towel to prevent them from drying out.

4 Lay one wrapper on a work surface in front of you and brush the edges with water. Put a teaspoonful of the crabmeat mixture in the center and fold the wrapper over the mixture to form a triangle.

5 Press the edges together to seal. Fold each side corner up to the top corner to make a small bundle, brushing the edges with water to seal if necessary. Repeat with the remaining wrappers and crabmeat mixture.

6 Heat the oil for deep-frying in the wok, a deep saucepan, or deep-fat fryer to 350–375°F, or until a cube of bread browns in 30 seconds.

7 Add the wontons, in batches, and cook for 45 seconds– 1 minute, until crisp and golden all over.

8 Remove with a slotted spoon, drain on paper towels, and keep warm while you cook the remaining wontons.

9 Serve with sweet chili dipping sauce.

08

Tempura Vegetables

SERVES 4

1 1/3 cups store-bought tempura mix

4 shiitake mushrooms

4 fresh asparagus spears

4 sweet potato slices

1 red bell pepper, seeded and
   cut into strips

4 onion slices, cut into rings

vegetable oil, for deep-frying

Dipping sauce

2 teaspoons mirin

1 tablespoon shoyu (Japanese
   soy sauce)

pinch of dashi granules, dissolved in
   2 tablespoons boiling water

Method

1 To make the dipping sauce, mix the ingredients together in a small dipping dish.

2 Mix the tempura with water according to the package directions.

3 Drop the vegetables into the batter.

4 Heat enough oil for deep-frying in a wok, deep-fat fryer, or large heavy saucepan until it reaches 350–375°F, or until a cube of bread browns in 30 seconds.

5 Lift 2–3 pieces of the vegetables out of the batter, add to the oil, and cook for 2–3 minutes, or until the batter is a light golden color.

6 Remove the tempura vegetables with a slotted spoon and drain on paper towels. Keep hot while you cook the remaining pieces. Transfer the tempura vegetables to a serving dish and serve with the dipping sauce.

09

Crispy "Seaweed"

SERVES 4

1/2 small head dark green
  cabbage

peanut oil or vegetable oil,
  for deep-frying

1 teaspoon sugar

1/2 teaspoon salt

1/4 cup slivered almonds, to garnish

Method

1 Remove and discard the tough stems from the cabbage leaves. Wash the leaves, drain thoroughly, and spread out on paper towels to dry.

2 Stack a few leaves and roll up tightly. Using a sharp knife, slice widthwise into the thinnest possible shreds. Repeat with the remaining leaves. Spread out the shreds on paper towels and let stand until completely dry.

3 Heat a large wok over high heat. Pour in the oil and heat to 350-375°F, or until a cube of bread browns in 30 seconds. Remove the wok from the heat and add half of the shredded leaves. Return the wok to the heat and deep-fry until the shreds begin to float to the surface and become crisp. Remove with a slotted spoon and drain on paper towels. Keep warm while you deep-fry the rest.

4 Transfer the shreds to a warm serving bowl. Combine the sugar and salt, and sprinkle over the "seaweed," tossing to mix.

5 Quickly cook the slivered almonds in the hot oil. Remove with a slotted spoon and sprinkle over the "seaweed." Serve warm or at room temperature.

10

Beef & Noodle Soup

SERVES 4

4 shallots, chopped

1 large garlic clove, chopped

2 teaspoons finely chopped
    fresh ginger

1 tablespoon peanut oil
    or vegetable oil

1 pound tenderloin steak, fat
    removed, cut into 1/2-inch cubes

51/2 cups beef stock

1 teaspoon white peppercorns,
    crushed

6 ounces flat rice noodles

juice of 1 lime

2 teaspoons Thai fish sauce

1/2 teaspoon salt

1/2 teaspoon sugar

To garnish

4 scallions, shredded

slivers of red chile

1/4 cup torn cilantro leaves

1/4 cup torn basil leaves

lime wedges

Method

1 Process the shallots, garlic, and ginger in a food processor or blender, pulsing several times until forming a smooth paste.

2 Heat a wok over medium–high heat, then add the oil and stir-fry the paste for 2 minutes, being careful to avoid letting it burn. Add the beef and stir-fry for 1 minute, until brown, then pour in 4 cups of the stock. Bring to a rolling boil, skimming off any foam that forms. Add the crushed peppercorns, then reduce the heat and gently simmer for 30–35 minutes, or until the meat is tender.

3 Meanwhile, soak the noodles in enough lukewarm water to cover for 15 minutes, or cook according to the package directions, until soft.

4 When the meat is tender, stir in any sticky residue that has formed at the edge of the wok. Add the remaining stock, the lime juice, fish sauce, salt, and sugar. Simmer for a few minutes.

5 Drain the noodles and divide among individual soup bowls. Ladle the meat and broth over the top. Serve with the garnishes sprinkled over the soup and lime wedges on the side.

11

Sweet & Sour Spareribs

SERVES 4

1 pound spareribs, cut into bite-size pieces

1 1/2 tablespoons peanut oil or vegetable oil, plus extra for deep-frying

1 green bell pepper, seeded and coarsely chopped

1 small onion, coarsely chopped

1 small carrot, finely sliced

1/2 teaspoon finely chopped garlic

1/2 teaspoon finely chopped fresh ginger

1/2 cup pineapple chunks

Marinade

2 teaspoons light soy sauce

1/2 teaspoon salt

pinch of white pepper

Sauce

3 tablespoons white rice vinegar

2 tablespoons sugar

1 tablespoon light soy sauce

1 tablespoon ketchup

Method

1 Combine all the marinade ingredients in a bowl. Add the spareribs and let marinate for at least 20 minutes.

2 Heat a large wok over high heat. Pour in the oil for deep-frying and heat to 350-375°F or until a cube of bread browns in 30 seconds.

3 Deep-fry the spareribs for 8 minutes. Drain and set aside.

4 To prepare the sauce, mix together the vinegar, sugar, light soy sauce, and ketchup. Set aside.

5 In the preheated wok, heat 1 tablespoon of the oil and stir-fry the bell pepper, onion, and carrot for 2 minutes. Remove and set aside. Wipe the wok clean and return to the heat.

6 In the clean, preheated wok, heat the remaining 1/2 tablespoon of oil and stir-fry the garlic and ginger until fragrant. Add the sauce. Bring back to a boil and add the pineapple chunks. Finally, add the spareribs and the reserved stir-fried vegetables. Stir until warmed through and serve immediately.

12

Chicken Noodle Soup

SERVES 4–6

8 ounces medium egg noodles

1 tablespoon vegetable oil

4 skinless, boneless chicken thighs, diced

1 bunch of scallions, sliced, white and green parts kept separate

2 garlic cloves, chopped

3/4-inch piece fresh ginger, finely chopped

3 1/2 cups chicken stock

3/4 cup coconut milk

1 tablespoon Thai red curry paste

3 tablespoons peanut butter

2 tablespoons light soy sauce

1 small red bell pepper, seeded and chopped

1/3 cup frozen peas

salt and pepper

Method

1 Cook the noodles in a saucepan of boiling water for 4 minutes, or according to the package directions, until soft. Drain, rinse under cold running water, and set aside.

2 Heat a wok over medium–high heat, then add the oil. Add the chicken and stir-fry for 5 minutes, or until lightly browned. Add the white part of the scallions, the garlic, and ginger and stir-fry for 2 minutes.

3 Add the stock, coconut milk, curry paste, peanut butter, and soy sauce. Season with salt and pepper. Bring to a boil, stirring continuously, then simmer for 8 minutes, stirring occasionally. Add the pepper, peas, and green scallion tops and cook for an additional 2 minutes.

4 Add the cooked noodles to the wok and heat through. Spoon into soup bowls and serve immediately.

13

Squid & Shrimp Laksa

SERVES 4

8 ounces dried wide rice noodles

3 cups coconut milk

2 fish bouillon cubes

3 fresh kaffir lime leaves

2 tablespoons Thai red curry paste

bunch of scallions,
  coarsely chopped

2 fresh red chiles, seeded and
  coarsely chopped

8 ounces fresh squid, cleaned and
  cut into rings

8 ounces large shrimp,
  peeled and deveined

handful of fresh cilantro, chopped,
  plus extra leaves to garnish

Method

1 Soak the noodles in a saucepan of boiling water for 4 minutes, covered, or cook according to the package directions, until tender. Drain, rinse under cold running water, and set aside.

2 Put the coconut milk, bouillon cubes, lime leaves, curry paste, scallions, and chiles in a wok and bring gently to a boil, stirring occasionally. Reduce the heat and simmer, stirring occasionally, for 2–3 minutes, until the bouillon cubes and paste have dissolved.

3 Add the squid and shrimp and simmer for 1–2 minutes, until the squid has plumped up and the shrimp have turned pink. Add the cooked noodles and the chopped cilantro and stir well. Ladle into individual bowls and serve immediately, garnished with cilantro leaves.

14

Hot & Sour Soup Tom Yum

SERVES 4

2 fresh red chiles, seeded
and coarsely chopped

1/3 cup rice vinegar

5 cups vegetable stock

2 lemongrass stalks, halved

1/4 cup soy sauce

1 tablespoon palm sugar
or brown sugar

juice of 1/2 lime

2 tablespoons peanut oil
or vegetable oil

1 1/2 cups cubed firm tofu
(1/2-inch cubes)

15-ounce can straw mushrooms,
drained

4 scallions, chopped

1 small head bok choy, shredded

Method

1 Mix the chiles and vinegar together in a nonmetallic bowl, cover, and let stand at room temperature for 1 hour.

2 Meanwhile, bring the stock to a boil in a saucepan. Add the lemongrass, soy sauce, sugar, and lime juice, reduce the heat, and simmer for 20–30 minutes.

3 Heat the oil in a preheated wok, add the tofu cubes, and stir-fry over high heat for 2–3 minutes, or until browned all over. (You may need to do this in two batches, depending on the size of the wok.)

4 Remove with a slotted spoon and drain on paper towels.

5 Add the chiles and vinegar with the tofu, mushrooms, and half of the scallions to the stock mixture and cook for 10 minutes.

6 Mix the remaining scallions with the bok choy.

7 Scatter over the scallions and bok choy and serve.

15

Thai-Style Seafood Soup

SERVES 4

5 1/2 cups fish stock

1 lemongrass stalk, split lengthwise

pared rind of 1/2 lime or
  1 fresh kaffir lime leaf

1-inch piece fresh ginger, sliced

1/4 teaspoon chili paste, or to taste

4–6 scallions

8 ounces large or medium shrimp,
  peeled and deveined

8 ounces scallops (16–20)

2 tablespoons cilantro leaves

salt

fresh red chile rings, to garnish

Method

1 Pour the stock into a wok with the lemongrass, lime rind, ginger, and chili paste. Bring just to a boil, then reduce the heat and simmer, covered, for 10–15 minutes.

2 Cut the scallions in half lengthwise, then slice widthwise thinly. Cut the shrimp almost in half lengthwise, keeping the tails intact.

3 Pour the stock through a strainer, then return to the wok and bring to a simmer, with bubbles rising at the edges and the surface trembling. Add the scallions and cook for 2–3 minutes. Taste and season with salt if needed. Stir in a little more chili paste if liked.

4 Add the scallops and shrimp and poach for 1 minute, or until the scallops turn opaque and the shrimp curl.

5 Drop in the cilantro leaves, then ladle the soup into bowls, dividing the shellfish evenly, and garnish with chile rings.

16

Mushroom & Ginger Soup

SERVES 4

1/2 ounce dried Chinese mushrooms

4 cups hot vegetable stock

4 ounces cellophane egg noodles

2 teaspoons sunflower oil

3 garlic cloves, crushed

1-inch piece fresh ginger,
   finely shredded

1/2 teaspoon ketchup

1 teaspoon light soy sauce

1 1/3 cups bean sprouts

fresh cilantro sprigs, to garnish

Method

1 Soak the dried Chinese mushrooms for at least 30 minutes in 1 1/4 cups of the hot stock. Drain the mushrooms and reserve the stock. Remove the stems of the mushrooms and discard. Slice the caps and reserve.

2 Cook the noodles according to the package directions. Drain well, rinse under cold water, and drain again. Set aside.

3 Heat the oil in a preheated wok or large skillet over high heat. Add the garlic and ginger, stir, and add the mushrooms. Stir over high heat for 2 minutes.

4 Add the remaining stock to the reserved stock and bring to a boil. Add the mushrooms, ketchup, and soy sauce. Stir in the bean sprouts and cook until tender.

5 Place some noodles in each soup bowl and ladle the soup on top. Garnish with fresh cilantro sprigs and serve immediately.

17

Rainbow Salad

SERVES 3–4

6 large shiitake mushrooms

10 scallions, green part included

6 carrots

3 tablespoons canola oil

1 red bell pepper, seeded
and finely sliced

8 ears of baby corn, halved
diagonally

3 cups fresh bean sprouts

salt

a few small mint leaves, to garnish

1/4 cup toasted coconut ribbons,
to garnish

Dressing

1/2 –1 green chile, seeded
and finely chopped

1 teaspoon sugar

1 1/2 teaspoons lime juice

2 teaspoons Thai fish sauce

2 tablespoons chopped mint

2 tablespoons canola oil

1/3 cup coconut milk

salt

Method

1 First make the dressing. Using a mortar and pestle, pound the chopped chile and the sugar to a watery green paste. Add the lime juice, fish sauce, and a pinch of salt, stirring to dissolve the sugar. Pour into a blender with the mint, oil, and coconut milk. Process until smooth and set aside.

2 Remove and discard the tough stems from the mushrooms, and thinly slice the caps. Halve the scallions lengthwise, then slice into 1-inch lengths, keeping the green and white parts separate.

3 Using a swivel vegetable peeler, shave the carrots into thin slivers. Heat a wok over high heat, then add the oil. Stir-fry the mushrooms, red bell pepper, baby corn, and the white scallions for 2 minutes. Add the carrots, bean sprouts, green scallions, and salt to taste. Toss for 1 minute until the vegetables are only just cooked and still crunchy.

4 Transfer to a colander set over a bowl to cool. Discard any drained liquid and transfer to a serving bowl. Toss with the dressing, then sprinkle with mint leaves and the toasted coconut ribbons. Serve at room temperature.

18

Chinese Chicken Salad

SERVES 4

3 boneless, skinless chicken breasts,
   about 1 pound in total, cut into
   bite-size pieces

2 teaspoons soy sauce

1/4 teaspoon freshly ground
   white pepper

2 tablespoons peanut oil or
   vegetable oil, plus extra for
   deep-frying

13/4 ounces thin rice noodles

1/2 head napa cabbage,
   thinly sliced diagonally

3 scallions, green parts included,
   sliced diagonally

1/3 cup whole almonds with skin,
   sliced lengthwise

2 teaspoons sesame seeds,
   to garnish

Dressing

1/3 cup olive oil

3 tablespoons rice vinegar

3 tablespoons light soy sauce

a few drops sesame oil

salt and pepper

Method

1 Sprinkle the chicken with the soy sauce and white pepper.
Combine the dressing ingredients and whisk to blend.

2 Heat a wok over high heat, then add the peanut oil.
Stir-fry the chicken for 4–5 minutes, until brown and crisp.
Drain on paper towels and let cool. Wipe out the wok.

3 Pour enough peanut oil for deep-frying into the wok. Heat
to 350-375°F or until a cube of bread browns in 30 seconds,
then fry a few noodles at a time until puffed up and crisp.
Drain on paper towels.

4 Arrange the sliced napa cabbage in a shallow serving dish.
Place the noodles in a pile on top of the cabbage on one side
of the dish. Arrange the chicken, scallions, and almonds
in the remaining space. Whisk the dressing again and pour over
the salad. Garnish with the sesame seeds and serve.

19

Gingered Chicken Salad

SERVES 4

4 skinless, boneless chicken breasts

4 scallions, chopped

1-inch piece fresh ginger,
   finely chopped

2 garlic cloves, crushed

2 tablespoons peanut oil
   or vegetable oil

Salad

1 tablespoon peanut oil
   or vegetable oil

1 onion, sliced

2 garlic cloves, chopped

8 ears of baby corn, halved

2 cups snow peas, halved lengthwise

1 red bell pepper, seeded and sliced

3-inch piece cucumber, peeled,
   seeded, and sliced

1/4 cup Thai soy sauce

1 tablespoon jaggery or
   light brown sugar

a few Thai basil leaves

6 ounces fine egg noodles

Method

1 Cut the chicken into 1-inch cubes. Mix the scallions, ginger, garlic, and oil together in a shallow dish and add the chicken. Cover and marinate in the refrigerator for at least 3 hours. Lift the meat out of the marinade and set aside.

2 Heat the oil in a wok, add the onion, and cook for 1–2 minutes. Add the garlic and the rest of the vegetables, except the cucumber, and cook for 2–3 minutes, until just tender. Add the cucumber, half of the soy sauce, the sugar, and basil, and mix gently.

3 Soak the noodles for 2–3 minutes, or according to the package directions, until tender, and drain well. Drizzle the remaining soy sauce over them and arrange on plates. Top with the cooked vegetables.

4 Add a little more oil to the wok, if necessary, add the chicken, and cook over a high heat until browned on all sides. Arrange the chicken on top of the salad and serve hot or warm.

20

Hot & Sour Vegetable Salad

SERVES 4

2 tablespoons peanut oil
   or vegetable oil

1 tablespoon chili oil

1 onion, sliced

1-inch piece fresh ginger, grated

1 small head broccoli,
   cut into florets

2 carrots, cut into short thin sticks

1 red bell pepper, seeded and cut
   into squares

1 yellow bell pepper, seeded and
   cut into strips

1 cup snow peas

4 ears of baby corn, halved

Dressing

2 tablespoons peanut oil
   or vegetable oil

1 teaspoon chili oil

1 tablespoon rice wine vinegar

juice of 1 lime

1/2 teaspoon Thai fish sauce

Method

1 Heat a wok over medium–high heat and add the oils. Sauté the onion and ginger for 1–2 minutes, until they start to soften. Add the vegetables and stir-fry for 2–3 minutes, until they have softened slightly. Remove from the heat and set aside.

2 Mix together the dressing ingredients. Transfer the vegetables to a serving plate and drizzle the dressing over. Serve warm immediately, or let the flavors develop and serve cold.

21

Spicy Crab & Shrimp Salad

SERVES 4

1 tablespoon peanut oil
or vegetable oil

1 fresh serrano chile, seeded and
finely chopped

2 cups snow peas, cut in half
diagonally

6 scallions, finely shredded

3 tablespoons frozen corn kernels,
thawed

6 ounces white crabmeat,
drained if canned

2 ounces shrimp, peeled
and deveined

1 carrot, grated

1¼ cups fresh bean sprouts

8 ounces baby spinach leaves,
trimmed

1 tablespoon finely grated
orange rind

2 tablespoons orange juice

1 tablespoon chopped fresh cilantro,
to garnish

Method

1 Heat a wok over medium heat, then add the oil. Add the chile and snow peas, then stir-fry for 2 minutes.

2 Add the scallions and corn kernels and continue to stir-fry for an additional minute.

3 Add the crabmeat, shrimp, carrot, bean sprouts, and spinach. Stir in the orange rind and juice and stir-fry for 2–3 minutes, or until the spinach has begun to wilt and everything is cooked.

4 Divide among four individual serving bowls, sprinkle with the cilantro, and serve immediately.

22

Gado Gado

SERVES 4

3 tablespoons peanut oil
  or vegetable oil

2 shallots, finely chopped

2 garlic cloves, crushed

1 red chile, finely chopped

juice of 2 limes

1 3/4 cup chunky peanut butter

1 cup coconut milk

2 cups beans

1/2 cucumber

1 red bell pepper

1 2/3 cups diced tempeh or firm tofu

2 cups bean sprouts

2 heads Boston lettuce, chopped

2 hard-boiled eggs, quartered

chopped cilantro, to garnish

Method

1 Heat a wok over medium heat and add 1 tablespoon of the oil. Cook the shallots and garlic for 2–3 minutes to soften but not brown.

2 Stir in the chile, lime juice, peanut butter, and coconut milk and stir over medium heat for 2–3 minutes. Remove from the wok and cool.

3 Cut the beans into bite-size pieces, then blanch in boiling water for 2 minutes. Drain and rinse in cold water.

4 Halve the cucumber lengthwise and slice diagonally. Seed and thinly slice the red bell pepper.

5 Heat the remaining oil in the wok and cook the tempeh until golden on all sides. Drain on paper towels.

6 Toss together the beans, cucumber, red bell pepper, bean sprouts, and lettuce and arrange on a large serving plate.

7 Arrange the fried tempeh and hard-boiled eggs over the salad.

8 Spoon the dressing onto the salad and sprinkle with chopped cilantro. Serve immediately.

MEAT

2

23

Sliced Beef in Black Bean Sauce

SERVES 4

3 tablespoons peanut oil
or vegetable oil

1 pound tenderloin steak,
thinly sliced

1 red bell pepper, seeded and
thinly sliced

1 green bell pepper, seeded
and thinly sliced

1 bunch scallions, sliced

2 garlic cloves, crushed

1 tablespoon grated fresh ginger

2 tablespoons black bean sauce

1 tablespoon dry sherry

1 tablespoon soy sauce

Method

1 Heat 2 tablespoons of the oil in a wok and stir-fry the beef over high heat for 1–2 minutes. Remove and set aside.

2 Add the remaining oil and bell peppers and stir-fry for 2 minutes. Remove and set aside.

3 Add the scallions, garlic, and ginger and stir-fry for 30 seconds.

4 Add the black bean sauce, sherry, and soy sauce, then stir in the beef and bell peppers and heat until bubbling.

5 Transfer to bowls and serve.

24

Beef Chow Mein

SERVES 4

12 ounces tenderloin steak,
  cut into slivers

8 ounces dried egg noodles

2 tablespoons peanut oil
  or vegetable oil

1 onion, finely sliced

1 green bell pepper, seeded
  and finely sliced

1 1/2 cups fresh bean sprouts

1 teaspoon salt

pinch of sugar

2 teaspoons Chinese rice wine

2 tablespoons light soy sauce

1 tablespoon dark soy sauce

1 tablespoon finely shredded scallion

Marinade

1 teaspoon light soy sauce

dash of sesame oil

1/2 teaspoon Chinese rice wine

pinch of white pepper

Method

1 Combine all the marinade ingredients in a bowl and marinate the beef for at least 20 minutes.

2 Cook the noodles according to the package directions. When cooked, rinse under cold water, drain, and set aside.

3 In a preheated wok or deep saucepan, heat the oil and stir-fry the steak for about 1 minute, until the meat has changed color, then add the onion and cook for 1 minute, followed by the bell pepper and bean sprouts. Let any water from the vegetables evaporate, then add the salt, sugar, rice wine, and soy sauces. Stir in the noodles and toss for 1 minute. Finally, stir in the scallion and serve.

25

Sichuan Peppered Beef

SERVES 4

1-inch piece fresh ginger, grated

1 garlic clove, crushed

*1 tablespoon Chinese rice wine
    or dry sherry*

1 tablespoon soy sauce

1 tablespoon hoisin sauce

*2 teaspoons crushed Sichuan
    peppercorns, without seeds*

1 pound tenderloin steak

*3 tablespoons peanut oil
    or vegetable oil*

1 onion, thinly sliced

*1 green bell pepper, seeded
    and thinly sliced*

Method

1 Mix together the ginger, garlic, rice wine, soy sauce, hoisin sauce, and peppercorns in a wide, nonmetallic bowl.

2 Thinly slice the steak into medallions and add to the bowl, turning to coat in the marinade. Cover and let marinate for 30 minutes.

3 Heat the oil in a wok and stir-fry the beef for 1–2 minutes to brown. Remove and keep to one side.

4 Add the onion and green bell pepper and stir-fry for 2 minutes. Add the beef with any marinade juices and stir to heat evenly.

5 Serve the beef immediately.

26

Beef Chop Suey

SERVES 4

1 pound rib-eye steak, sliced

1 head broccoli, cut into florets

2 tablespoons vegetable oil

1 onion, sliced

2 celery stalks, sliced

3 1/2 cups snow peas,
  sliced lengthwise

1/2 cup of canned bamboo shoots,
  rinsed and shredded

8 water chestnuts, sliced

3 cups sliced white button
  mushrooms

1 tablespoon oyster sauce

1 teaspoon salt

Marinade

1 tablespoon Chinese rice wine
  or dry sherry

1/2 teaspoon white pepper

1/2 teaspoon salt

1 tablespoon light soy sauce

1/2 teaspoon sesame oil

Method

1 Combine all the marinade ingredients in a bowl and marinate the beef for at least 20 minutes.

2 Blanch the broccoli in a large saucepan of boiling water for 30 seconds. Drain and set aside.

3 In a preheated wok, heat 1 tablespoon of the oil and stir-fry the beef until the color has changed. Remove and set aside.

4 Clean the wok, heat the remaining oil, and stir-fry the onion for 1 minute. Add the celery and broccoli and cook for 2 minutes. Add the snow peas, bamboo shoots, water chestnuts, and mushrooms and cook for 1 minute. Add the beef and season with the oyster sauce and salt.

5 Transfer to bowls and serve.

27

Hot Sesame Beef

SERVES 4

*1 pound tenderloin steak,
   cut into thin strips*

1 1/2 tablespoons sesame seeds

1/2 cup beef stock

2 tablespoons soy sauce

2 tablespoons grated fresh ginger

2 garlic cloves, finely chopped

1 teaspoon cornstarch

1/2 teaspoon crushed red pepper

3 tablespoons sesame oil

1 large head broccoli, cut into florets

*1 yellow bell pepper, seeded
   and thinly sliced*

1 red chile, seeded and finely sliced

1 tablespoon chili oil, to taste

cooked wild rice, to serve

*1 tablespoon chopped fresh cilantro,
   to garnish*

Method

1 Mix the beef strips with 1 tablespoon of the sesame seeds in a small bowl. In a separate bowl, whisk together the beef stock, soy sauce, ginger, garlic, cornstarch, and crushed red peppers.

2 Heat 1 tablespoon of the sesame oil in a large wok or skillet. Stir-fry the beef strips for 2–3 minutes. Remove and set aside.

3 Discard any remaining oil in the wok, then wipe with paper towels to remove any stray sesame seeds. Heat the remaining oil, add the broccoli, bell pepper, crushed red pepper, and chili oil and stir-fry for 2–3 minutes. Stir in the beef stock mixture, cover, and simmer for 2 minutes.

4 Return the beef to the wok and simmer until the juices thicken, stirring occasionally. Cook for another 1–2 minutes.

5 Sprinkle with the remaining sesame seeds. Serve over freshly cooked wild rice and garnish with fresh cilantro.

28

Marinated Beef with Vegetables

SERVES 4

*1 pound top sirloin steak,
    cut into thin strips*

3 tablespoons sesame oil

1/2 tablespoon cornstarch

1/2 tablespoon soy sauce

1 head broccoli, cut into florets

2 carrots, cut into thin strips

2 cups snow peas

1/2 cup beef stock

9 ounces baby spinach, shredded

*freshly cooked plain rice or noodles,
    to serve*

Marinade

1 tablespoon dry sherry

1/2 tablespoon soy sauce

1/2 tablespoon cornstarch

1/2 teaspoon sugar

2 garlic cloves, finely chopped

1 tablespoon sesame oil

Method

1 To make the marinade, mix the sherry, soy sauce, cornstarch, sugar, garlic, and oil in a bowl. Add the beef to the mixture and cover with plastic wrap. Set aside to marinate for 30 minutes, then remove the beef and discard the marinade.

2 Heat a wok over medium–high heat, then add 1 tablespoon of the oil. Stir-fry the beef for 2 minutes, until medium–rare. Remove from the wok and set aside.

3 Combine the cornstarch and soy sauce in a bowl and set aside. Pour the remaining 2 tablespoons of oil into the wok, add the broccoli, carrots, and snow peas, and stir-fry for 2 minutes.

4 Add the stock, cover the wok, and cook for 1 minute. Stir in the spinach, beef, and the cornstarch mixture. Cook until the juices boil and thicken. Serve with cooked rice or noodles.

29

Ginger Beef with Yellow Peppers

SERVES 4

1 pound tenderloin steak,
    cut into 1-inch cubes

2 teaspoons peanut oil
    or vegetable oil

2 garlic cloves, crushed

2 tablespoons grated fresh ginger

pinch of crushed red pepper

2 yellow bell peppers, seeded
    and thinly sliced

8 ears of baby corn

3 cups snow peas

freshly cooked rice noodles drizzled
    with sesame oil, to serve

Marinade

2 tablespoons soy sauce

2 teaspoons peanut oil
    or vegetable oil

1½ teaspoons sugar

1 teaspoon cornstarch

Method

1 To make the marinade, mix the soy sauce, oil, sugar, and cornstarch in a bowl. Stir in the beef, then cover with plastic wrap and set aside to marinate for 30 minutes.

2 Heat a wok over medium–high heat, then add the oil. Add the garlic, ginger, and crushed red pepper and cook for 30 seconds. Stir in the yellow bell peppers and baby corn, and stir-fry for 2 minutes. Add the snow peas and cook for another minute.

3 Remove the vegetables from the wok. Add the beef and marinade to the wok and stir-fry for 3–4 minutes, or until cooked to taste. Return the vegetables to the wok, mix well, and cook until all the ingredients are heated through. Remove from the heat and serve with cooked noodles.

30

Beef & Bok Choy Stir-Fry

SERVES 4

12 ounces skirt steak

2 tablespoons peanut oil
or vegetable oil

1 shallot, chopped

2 teaspoons finely chopped
fresh ginger

1 fresh red chile, seeded and
thinly sliced

1/2 head bok choy, stems cut into
1-inch pieces and leaves sliced
into wide ribbons

1 tablespoon cornstarch

2 tablespoons beef stock or water

1/4 cup chopped fresh cilantro,
to garnish

Marinade

2 tablespoons soy sauce

1 1/2 tablespoons Chinese rice wine
or dry sherry

1/2 teaspoon sugar

1/2 teaspoon pepper

1/4 teaspoon salt

Method

1 Pound the steak with the blunt side of a knife. Slice
diagonally across the grain into thin bite-size pieces and
put in a shallow bowl.

2 Combine the marinade ingredients in a bowl and pour over
the beef, stirring to coat. Let marinate for 1 hour at room
temperature, or overnight in the refrigerator.

3 Heat a wok over medium–high heat, then add the oil. Stir-fry
the shallot, ginger, and chile for 1 minute. Increase the heat to
high and add the beef and marinade. Stir-fry for 3 minutes. Add
the bok choy stems and stir-fry for 1 minute. Add the leaves and
stir-fry for another minute.

4 Mix the cornstarch and stock to a smooth paste. Add to
the wok and stir-fry for 1 minute, until slightly thickened.
Transfer to a warm serving dish and garnish with the cilantro.
Serve immediately.

31

Beef with Mixed Mushrooms

SERVES 2–3

1 1/2 tablespoons Sichuan peppers

1/2 teaspoon salt

12 ounces top sirloin steak

7 ounces mixed small mushrooms, such as cremini, enoki, and buna shimeji

1/2 tablespoon cornstarch

1/2 cup beef stock

2 teaspoons Chinese rice wine or dry sherry

4 teaspoons soy sauce

3 tablespoons peanut oil or vegetable oil

1 shallot, finely chopped

1 teaspoon finely chopped fresh ginger

1 large garlic clove, thinly sliced

3 tablespoons chopped fresh cilantro, to garnish

Method

1 Place the Sichuan peppers in a mortar with the salt and grind with a pestle. Sprinkle over both sides of the meat, pressing in well. Slice the meat diagonally across the grain into thin bite-size pieces and set aside.

2 Wipe the mushrooms with damp paper towels. If using clumping mushrooms, such as enoki and buna shimeji, cut off the root and separate the clump. Cut any large mushrooms in half.

3 Mix the cornstarch to a paste with 2 tablespoons of the stock. Add the rice wine and soy sauce, mixing well.

4 Heat a wok over medium–high heat, then add 1 tablespoon of the oil. Cook the shallot and ginger for 1 minute. Add the garlic and cook for a few seconds, then add the mushrooms and 2 tablespoons of the stock. Stir-fry for 4 minutes. Add the cornstarch mixture and the remaining stock. Bring to a boil, stirring, then reduce the heat and simmer for 2 minutes. Transfer to a warm serving dish.

5 Wipe out the wok with paper towels, then heat over high heat. Add the remaining oil. Add the beef and stir-fry for 3 minutes. Add to the mushroom mixture and garnish with the cilantro. Serve immediately.

32

Marinated Beef with Celery

SERVES 4

*1 pound tenderloin steak,
cut into thin strips*

*1 cup plus 2 tablespoons
vegetable oil*

*3 celery stalks, cut into thin
1-inch-long strips*

1 red bell pepper, cut into thin strips

1 red chile, seeded and finely sliced

lime wedges, to garnish

Thai fish sauce, to serve

Marinade

1 teaspoon salt

2 tablespoons Thai fish sauce

Method

1 To make the marinade, mix the salt and fish sauce in a large bowl.

2 Add the beef to the marinade and toss to coat. Cover with plastic wrap and place in the refrigerator for 1 hour to marinate.

3 Heat 1 cup of the oil in a wok, add the beef, and deep-fry over medium heat for 2–3 minutes until crispy. Remove the wok from the heat and, using a slotted spoon, lift out the meat and drain it on paper towels. Discard all but 2 tablespoons of the oil.

4 Add the remaining oil to the wok. When it is hot add the celery, red bell pepper, and chile and stir-fry for 1 minute. Add the beef and cook until hot.

5 Garnish with lime wedges and serve with fish sauce.

33

Lamb with Black Bean Sauce

SERVES 4

1 pound boneless lamb shoulder
   or boneless leg of lamb

1 egg white, lightly beaten

1/4 cup cornstarch

1 teaspoon five-spice powder

3 tablespoons sunflower oil

1 red onion, sliced

1 red bell pepper, seeded and sliced

1 green bell pepper, seeded and
   sliced

1 yellow or orange bell pepper,
   seeded and sliced

1/3 cup black bean sauce

cooked rice or noodles,
   to serve

Method

1 Using a sharp knife, slice the lamb into thin strips.

2 Mix together the egg white, cornstarch, and five-spice powder. Toss the lamb strips in the mixture until evenly coated.

3 Heat the oil in a wok or skillet and stir-fry the lamb over high heat for 5 minutes, or until it crispens around the edges.

4 Add the onion and bell pepper slices to the wok and stir-fry for 5–6 minutes, or until the vegetables just begin to soften.

5 Stir the black bean sauce into the mixture in the wok and heat through.

6 Transfer the lamb and sauce to warm serving plates and serve hot with freshly cooked rice or noodles.

34

Stir-Fried Lamb with Orange

SERVES 4

1 pound fresh ground lamb

2 garlic cloves, crushed

1 teaspoon cumin seeds

1 teaspoon ground coriander

1 red onion, sliced

finely grated rind and juice
   of 1 orange

2 tablespoons soy sauce

1 orange, peeled and segmented

salt and pepper

snipped fresh chives and strips of
   orange zest, to garnish

Method

1 Heat a wok without adding any oil. Add the ground lamb and dry-fry for 5 minutes, or until evenly browned. Drain away any excess fat from the wok.

2 Add the garlic, cumin seeds, coriander, and red onion to the wok and stir-fry for another 5 minutes.

3 Stir in the orange rind and juice and the soy sauce, mixing until thoroughly combined. Cover, reduce the heat, and let simmer, stirring occasionally, for 15 minutes.

4 Remove the lid, increase the heat, and add the orange segments. Stir to mix.

5 Season with salt and pepper and heat through for an additional 2–3 minutes. Transfer the stir-fry to warm serving dishes and garnish with snipped chives and strips of orange zest. Serve immediately.

35

Green Lamb Stir-Fry

SERVES 4

1 pound boneless lamb

2 tablespoons soy sauce

2 teaspoons cornstarch

1 cup chicken stock

1 tablespoon Thai fish sauce

4 ounces Chinese garlic chives,
 or green stems from 2 bunches
 of scallions

4 1/2 ounces dried egg noodles

3 tablespoons peanut oil
 or vegetable oil

3/4-inch piece galangal or fresh
 ginger, finely chopped

1/3 cup green curry paste

1/3 cup coarsely chopped,
 dry-roasted peanuts and
 juice of 1/2 lime, to garnish

salt

lime slices, to serve

Method

1 Slice the lamb into 1 1/2 x 1/2-inch strips and put in a shallow dish. Sprinkle with the soy sauce, cornstarch, and a pinch of salt, tossing well to coat. Cover and let marinate in the refrigerator for 1–24 hours.

2 Combine the stock, fish sauce, and 1/2 teaspoon of salt. Trim the garlic chives and slice into 3/4-inch lengths.

3 Cook the noodles according to the package directions. Drain, return to the saucepan, and toss with 1 tablespoon of the oil.

4 Heat a wok over high heat. Add the remaining oil and stir-fry the lamb for 3 minutes, or until no longer pink. Add the galangal and curry paste and stir for another minute. Pour in the stock mixture and stir until boiling. Add the noodles, tossing to coat with the sauce. Add the chives and stir-fry for a few seconds until wilted. Garnish with the peanuts and lime juice, and serve immediately with lime slices.

36

Red Lamb Curry

SERVES 4

2 tablespoons vegetable oil

1 large onion, sliced

2 garlic cloves, crushed

1 pound lean boneless leg of lamb,
   cut into 1½-inch cubes

2 tablespoons red curry paste

2/3 cup coconut milk

1 tablespoon light brown sugar

1 large red bell pepper, seeded and
   thickly sliced

2/3 cup lamb stock or beef stock

1 tablespoon Thai fish sauce

2 tablespoons lime juice

8-ounce can water chestnuts,
   drained

2 tablespoons chopped fresh cilantro

2 tablespoons chopped fresh basil,
   plus extra leaves to garnish

salt and pepper

Method

1 Heat a wok over high heat, then add the oil. Add the onion
and garlic and stir-fry for 2–3 minutes, until soft. Add the lamb
and stir-fry quickly until lightly browned.

2 Stir in the curry paste and cook for a few seconds, then add the
coconut milk and sugar and bring to a boil. Reduce the heat and let
simmer for 15 minutes, stirring occasionally.

3 Stir in the red bell pepper, stock, fish sauce, and lime juice,
then cover and simmer for another 15 minutes, or until the
lamb is tender.

4 Add the water chestnuts, cilantro, and chopped basil and season
with salt and pepper. Transfer to serving plates, then garnish with
basil leaves and serve immediately.

37

Sweet & Sour Pork

SERVES 4

2/3 cup vegetable oil, for deep-frying

8 ounces pork tenderloin,
 cut into 1/2-inch cubes

1 onion, sliced

1 green bell pepper, seeded
 and sliced

8-ounce can pineapple pieces, drained

1 small carrot, cut into thin strips

1/4 cup of canned bamboo shoots,
 drained, rinsed, and halved

cooked rice or noodles, to serve

Batter

1 cup all-purpose flour

1 tablespoon cornstarch

1 1/2 teaspoons baking powder

1 tablespoon vegetable oil

Sauce

1/2 cup firmly packed light brown sugar

2 tablespoons cornstarch

1/2 cup white wine vinegar

2 garlic cloves, crushed

1/4 cup tomato paste

1/3 cup pineapple juice

Method

1 To make the batter, sift the all-purpose flour into a mixing bowl, together with the cornstarch and baking powder. Add the vegetable oil and stir in enough water to make about 3/4 cup of a thick, smooth batter.

2 Pour the vegetable oil into a preheated wok and heat until almost smoking.

3 Dip the cubes of pork into the batter and cook in the hot oil, in batches, until the pork is cooked through. Remove the pork from the wok with a slotted spoon and drain on paper towels. Set aside and keep warm until required.

4 Drain all but 1 tablespoon of oil from the wok and return it to the heat. Add the onion, bell pepper, pineapple pieces, carrot, and bamboo shoots and stir-fry for 1–2 minutes. Remove from the wok with a slotted spoon and set aside.

5 Mix all of the sauce ingredients together and pour into the wok. Bring to a boil, stirring until thickened and clear. Cook for 1 minute, then return the pork and vegetables to the wok. Cook for another 1–2 minutes, then transfer to a serving plate and serve with freshly cooked rice or noodles.

38

Honey-Glazed Roast Pork

SERVES 4

2 teaspoons five-spice powder

1 small garlic clove, crushed

4 teaspoons light soy sauce

2 tablespoons honey

1 tablespoon rice vinegar

2 tablespoons firmly packed light
  brown sugar

1 tablespoon hoisin sauce

1 pound pork tenderloin,
  in one piece

3 tablespoons rice wine

1 teaspoon cornstarch

3/4 cup chicken stock

stir-fried vegetables, to serve

Method

1 Mix together the five-spice powder, crushed garlic, and 1 teaspoon of the soy sauce to form a five-spice paste.

2 Mix together the honey, vinegar, sugar, hoisin sauce, remaining soy sauce, and five-spice paste in a separate wide, nonmetallic bowl. Pour over the pork. Cover and let marinate in the refrigerator overnight.

3 Preheat the oven to 400°F. Drain the pork, reserving the marinade, and place on a wire rack in a roasting pan.

4 Pour a 1-inch depth of boiling water into the pan and place in the oven for 20 minutes.

5 Turn the pork over, brush with the marinade, then cook for another 20 minutes, or until there is no trace of pink in the juices.

6 Mix the rice wine and cornstarch to a smooth paste, then place in a saucepan with the reserved marinade and stock.

7 Bring to boiling point, while stirring, then simmer for 2 minutes, until thickened and clear.

8 Slice the pork thinly and serve with the sauce spooned over. Serve with stir-fried vegetables.

39

Pork with Basil & Lemongrass

SERVES 4

12 ounces pork tenderloin, cubed

2 tablespoons sesame oil

4 cups thinly sliced white button mushrooms

1 zucchini, thinly sliced

2 carrots, thinly sliced

1 cup of canned bamboo shoots, drained and rinsed

1 cup of canned water chestnuts, thinly sliced

1 garlic clove, crushed

1/2 cup chicken stock

lime wedges, to serve

cooked basmati rice, to serve

Marinade

1 lemongrass stalk, finely sliced

2 tablespoons Thai fish sauce

1/4 cup fresh basil, shredded

juice of 1 lime

Method

1 To make the marinade, mix the lemongrass, fish sauce, basil, and lime juice in a bowl. Stir in the pork and toss well to coat. Cover with plastic wrap and refrigerate for 1–2 hours.

2 Heat 1 tablespoon of the oil in a preheated wok or skillet over medium heat. Add the meat and the marinade and stir-fry until the pork is browned. Remove from the wok, set aside, and keep warm.

3 Add the remaining tablespoon of oil to the wok and heat. Add all the vegetables and the garlic and stir-fry for about 3 minutes.

4 Return the pork to the wok and add the chicken stock. Cook for 5 minutes, until the stock is reduced.

5 Transfer the stir-fry to warm serving dishes. Serve with lime wedges and freshly cooked basmati rice.

40

Pad Noodles with Pork & Shrimp

SERVES 4

8 ounces flat rice noodles

8 ounces pork tenderloin

3 tablespoons peanut oil
    or vegetable oil

2 shallots, finely chopped

2 garlic cloves, finely chopped

6 ounces shrimp, peeled and
    deveined

2 eggs, beaten

2 tablespoons Thai fish sauce

juice of 1 lime

1 tablespoon ketchup

2 teaspoons light brown sugar

1/2 teaspoon crushed red pepper

1 cup bean sprouts

1/4 cup roasted salted peanuts,
    chopped

6 scallions, diagonally sliced

Method

1 Soak the noodles in hot water for 10 minutes, or according to the package directions. Drain well.

2 Slice the pork into strips about 1/4 inch thick.

3 Heat the oil in a wok and stir-fry the shallots for 1–2 minutes, to soften.

4 Add the pork strips and stir-fry for 2–3 minutes.

5 Add the garlic and shrimp and stir-fry for 1–2 minutes.

6 Pour in the beaten eggs and stir for a few seconds until lightly set.

7 Reduce the heat and add the noodles, fish sauce, lime juice, ketchup, and sugar. Toss together and heat through.

8 Sprinkle with crushed red pepper, bean sprouts, peanuts, and scallions.

9 Transfer to bowls and serve.

41

Hoisin Pork with Garlic Noodles

SERVES 4

*8 ounces dried thick Chinese egg
noodles, or Chinese whole-wheat
egg noodles*

*1 pound pork tenderloin,
thinly sliced*

1 teaspoon sugar

*1 tablespoon peanut oil
or vegetable oil*

¼ cup rice vinegar

¼ cup white wine vinegar

¼ cup hoisin sauce

2 scallions, sliced diagonally

*about 2 tablespoons garlic-flavored
vegetable oil*

2 large garlic cloves, thinly sliced

chopped fresh cilantro, to garnish

Method

1 Boil the noodles for 3 minutes, until soft, or cook according
to the package directions. Drain well, rinse under cold water, and
drain again, then set aside.

2 Meanwhile, sprinkle the pork slices with the sugar and use
your hands to toss together. Heat a wok over high heat. Add the
oil and heat until it shimmers. Add the pork and stir-fry for about
3 minutes, until the pork is cooked through and is no longer pink.
Use a slotted spoon to remove the pork from the wok and keep
warm. Add both vinegars to the wok and boil until they are reduced
to about ⅓ cup. Pour in the hoisin sauce with the scallions and let
it bubble until reduced by half. Add to the pork and stir together.

3 Quickly wipe out the wok and reheat. Add the garlic-flavored oil
and heat until it shimmers. Add the garlic slices and stir for about
30 seconds, until they are golden and crisp, then use a slotted
spoon to scoop them out of the wok and set aside.

4 Add the noodles to the wok and stir to warm them through.
Divide the noodles among four plates, top with the pork-and-onion
mixture, and garnish with the garlic slices and cilantro.

42

Ginger Pork with Mushrooms

SERVES 4

2 tablespoons vegetable oil

3 shallots, finely chopped

2 garlic cloves, crushed

2-inch piece fresh ginger,
thinly sliced

1 pound pork, cut into strips

9 ounces shiitake mushrooms, sliced

¼ cup soy sauce

¼ cup rice wine

1 teaspoon light brown sugar

1 teaspoon cornstarch

2 tablespoons cold water

3 tablespoons chopped fresh
cilantro, to garnish

Method

1 Heat the oil in a wok and cook the shallots for 2–3 minutes,
to soften.

2 Add the garlic and ginger and stir-fry for 1 minute.

3 Add the pork strips and stir-fry for 1 minute.

4 Add the mushrooms and stir-fry for another 2–3 minutes.

5 Stir in the soy sauce, rice wine, and sugar.

6 Blend the cornstarch and water until smooth, add to the wok,
stirring, and cook until the juices are thickened and clear.

7 Serve the stir-fry garnished with cilantro.

POULTRY

43

Green Chicken Curry

SERVES 4

2 tablespoons peanut oil or
sunflower oil

2 tablespoons green curry paste

1 pound skinless, boneless chicken
breasts, cut into cubes

2 kaffir lime leaves, coarsely torn

1 lemongrass stalk, finely chopped

1 cup coconut milk

16 baby eggplants, halved

2 tablespoons Thai fish sauce

fresh Thai basil sprigs and thinly
sliced kaffir lime leaves, to garnish

Method

1 Heat the oil in a preheated wok or large, heavy skillet. Add the curry paste and stir-fry briefly until all the aromas are released.

2 Add the chicken, lime leaves, and lemongrass and stir-fry for 3–4 minutes, until the meat is beginning to color. Add the coconut milk and eggplants and simmer gently for 8–10 minutes, or until tender.

3 Stir in the fish sauce and serve immediately, garnished with basil sprigs and sliced lime leaves.

44

Chicken Chow Mein

SERVES 4

8 ounces medium egg noodles

2 tablespoons sunflower oil

2 cups shredded, cooked
   chicken breasts

1 garlic clove, finely chopped

1 red bell pepper, seeded and
   thinly sliced

4 ounces shiitake mushrooms, sliced

6 scallions, sliced

1 cup bean sprouts

3 tablespoons soy sauce

1 tablespoon sesame oil

Method

1 Place the egg noodles in a large bowl or dish and break them up slightly. Pour enough boiling water over the noodles to cover and let stand while preparing the other ingredients. Alternatively, prepare according to the package directions.

2 Heat the sunflower oil in a large preheated wok. Add the chicken, garlic, red bell pepper, mushrooms, scallions, and bean sprouts to the wok and stir-fry for about 5 minutes.

3 Drain the noodles thoroughly. Add the noodles to the wok, toss well and stir-fry for another 5 minutes.

4 Drizzle the soy sauce and sesame oil over the chow mein and toss until well combined.

5 Transfer to warm serving bowls and serve immediately.

45

Chicken with Cashew Nuts

SERVES 4–6

1 pound boneless chicken, cut into
  bite-size pieces

3 tablespoons light soy sauce

1 teaspoon Chinese rice wine

pinch of sugar

1/2 teaspoon salt

3 dried Chinese mushrooms, soaked
  in warm water for 20 minutes

2 tablespoons peanut oil
  or vegetable oil

4 slices of fresh ginger

1 teaspoon finely chopped garlic

1 red bell pepper, seeded and cut
  into 1-inch squares

3/4 cup cashew nuts, toasted

Method

1 Marinate the chicken in 2 tablespoons of the light soy sauce, rice wine, sugar, and salt for at least 20 minutes.

2 Squeeze any excess water from the mushrooms and finely slice, discarding any tough stems. Reserve the soaking water.

3 In a preheated wok, heat 1 tablespoon of the oil. Add the ginger and stir-fry until fragrant. Stir in the chicken and cook for 2 minutes, until it turns brown. Before the chicken is cooked through, remove and set aside.

4 Clean the wok, heat the remaining oil, and stir-fry the garlic until fragrant. Add the mushrooms and red bell pepper and stir-fry for 1 minute.

5 Add about 2 tablespoons of the mushroom soaking water and cook for about 2 minutes, until the water has evaporated.

6 Return the chicken to the wok, add the remaining light soy sauce and the cashew nuts, and stir-fry for 2 minutes, until the chicken is cooked through.

7 Transfer to bowls and serve.

46

Sweet & Sour Chicken

SERVES 4–6

1 pound lean chicken, cubed

1/3 cup peanut oil or vegetable

1/2 teaspoon crushed garlic

1/2 teaspoon finely chopped
  fresh ginger

1 green bell pepper, seeded and
  coarsely chopped

1 onion, coarsely chopped

1 carrot, finely sliced

1 teaspoon sesame oil

1 tablespoon finely chopped scallion

freshly cooked rice, to serve

Marinade

2 teaspoons light soy sauce

1 teaspoon Chinese rice wine or
  dry sherry

pinch of white pepper

1/2 teaspoon salt

dash of sesame oil

Sauce

1/2 cup rice vinegar

1/4 cup sugar

2 teaspoons light soy sauce

1/3 cup ketchup

Method

1 Combine all the marinade ingredients in a bowl and marinate the chicken pieces for at least 20 minutes.

2 To prepare the sauce, heat the vinegar in a saucepan and add the sugar, light soy sauce, and ketchup. Stir to dissolve the sugar, then set aside.

3 In a preheated wok or large skillet, heat 3 tablespoons of the oil and stir-fry the chicken until it starts to turn golden brown. Remove and set aside. Wipe the wok clean.

4 In the clean wok, heat the remaining oil and cook the garlic and ginger until fragrant. Add the vegetables and cook for 2 minutes. Add the chicken and cook for 1 minute. Finally, add the sauce and the sesame oil, then stir in the scallion and serve immediately with freshly cooked rice.

47

Yaki Soba

SERVES 2

14 ounces ramen noodles

1 onion, finely sliced

2 cups bean sprouts

1 red bell pepper, seeded and sliced

1 cup sliced, cooked chicken

12 cooked, peeled shrimp

1 tablespoon oil, for stir-frying

2 tablespoons shoyu
(Japanese soy sauce)

1/2 tablespoon mirin

1 teaspoon sesame oil

1 teaspoon sesame seeds and
2 scallions, finely sliced,
to garnish

Method

1 Cook the noodles according to the package directions, drain well, and transfer to a bowl.

2 Mix the onion, bean sprouts, red bell pepper, chicken, and shrimp together in a bowl. Stir through the noodles. Meanwhile, preheat a wok over high heat, add the oil, and heat until very hot.

3 Add the noodle mixture and stir-fry for 4 minutes, or until golden. Add the shoyu, mirin, and sesame oil and toss together.

4 Divide the noodles between two bowls.

5 Sprinkle with sesame seeds and scallions and serve.

48

Peppered Chicken Stir-Fry

SERVES 4–6

4 teaspoons soy sauce

1 tablespoon cornstarch

1 tablespoon Chinese rice wine or dry sherry

1/4 teaspoon salt

12 ounces skinless, boneless chicken breasts, cut into cubes

1/3 cup chicken stock

1 tablespoon oyster sauce

1/4 cup peanut oil or vegetable oil

1 teaspoon finely chopped fresh ginger

1 large garlic clove, thinly sliced

4 scallions, white and green parts separated, diagonally sliced into 3/4-inch pieces

1/2 tablespoon white peppercorns, crushed

8 ears of baby corn, diagonally halved

1/2 small red bell pepper, seeded and thinly sliced

1 cup of canned water chestnuts, drained

2 cups snow peas, diagonally halved

Method

1 In a small bowl, combine half of the soy sauce, the cornstarch, rice wine, and salt. Put the chicken pieces in a shallow dish and pour over the soy sauce mixture, stirring to coat. Let stand for 15 minutes.

2 Mix the remaining soy sauce with the stock and oyster sauce and set aside.

3 Heat a wok over high heat, then add the oil. Add the chicken and stir-fry for 3 minutes, until no longer pink. Remove from the wok with a slotted spoon and drain on paper towels.

4 Reduce the heat slightly, then add the ginger, garlic, white scallions, and the crushed peppercorns and stir for a few seconds. Add the baby corn, red bell pepper, and water chestnuts. Stir-fry for 2 minutes, then return the chicken to the wok. Add the snow peas and the soy sauce mixture and stir-fry for 1–2 minutes, until the sauce is thickened.

5 Sprinkle with the green scallion and cook for a few seconds. Serve immediately.

49

Teriyaki Chicken

SERVES 4

4 boneless chicken breasts, about 6 ounces each, with or without skin

1/4 cup teriyaki sauce, plus extra for brushing

peanut oil or vegetable oil, for brushing

Sesame noodles

8 ounces dried thin buckwheat noodles

1 tablespoon toasted sesame oil

2 tablespoons sesame seeds, toasted

2 tablespoons finely chopped fresh parsley

salt and pepper

Method

1 Using a sharp knife, score each chicken breast diagonally across three times. Rub all over with the teriyaki sauce. Set aside in the refrigerator to marinate for at least 10 minutes and up to 24 hours.

2 Preheat the broiler to high. Bring a saucepan of water to a boil, add the buckwheat noodles, and cook according to the package directions. Drain and rinse well in cold water.

3 Lightly brush the broiler pan with oil. Add the chicken breasts, skin side up.

4 Broil the chicken breasts, brushing occasionally with extra teriyaki sauce, for 15 minutes, or until cooked through and the juices run clear when pierced with the tip of a sharp knife.

5 Meanwhile, heat a wok over high heat. Add the sesame oil and heat until it shimmers.

6 Add the noodles and stir to heat through, then stir in the sesame seeds and parsley. Add salt and pepper to taste. Transfer the chicken breasts to plates and divide the noodles among them.

50

Gong Bau Chicken

SERVES 4

2 boneless chicken breasts, with
or without skin, cut into
1/2-inch cubes

1 tablespoon peanut oil
or vegetable oil

10 dried red chiles, or to taste,
snipped into 2–3 pieces

1 teaspoon Sichuan peppers

3 garlic cloves, finely sliced

1-inch piece fresh ginger, finely sliced

1 tablespoon coarsely chopped
scallion, white part only

1/2 cup peanuts, roasted

Marinade

2 teaspoons light soy sauce

1 teaspoon Chinese rice wine

1/2 teaspoon sugar

Sauce

1 teaspoon light soy sauce

1 teaspoon dark soy sauce

1 teaspoon black rice vinegar

a few drops of sesame oil

2 tablespoons chicken stock

1 teaspoon sugar

Method

1 Combine all the marinade ingredients in a bowl and marinate the chicken, covered, for at least 20 minutes. Combine all the ingredients for the sauce and set aside.

2 In a preheated wok or large skillet, heat the oil and stir-fry the chiles and Sichuan peppers until crisp and fragrant. Toss in the chicken pieces. When they begin to turn white, add the garlic, ginger, and scallion. Stir-fry for about 5 minutes, or until the chicken is cooked.

3 Pour in the sauce, mix together thoroughly, then stir in the peanuts. Serve immediately.

51

Chicken with Pistachio Nuts

SERVES 4

1/4 cup chicken stock

2 tablespoons soy sauce

2 tablespoons dry sherry

1 tablespoon cornstarch

1 egg white, beaten

1/2 teaspoon salt

1/4 cup peanut oil or vegetable oil

1 pound chicken breast,
   cut into strips

6 1/2 cups thinly sliced white button
   mushrooms (about 1 pound)

1 head broccoli, cut into florets

1 1/2 cups bean sprouts

1 cup of canned water chestnuts,
   drained and thinly sliced

1 1/3 cups pistachio nuts,
   plus extra to garnish

cooked rice, to serve

Method

1 Combine the chicken stock, soy sauce, and sherry with 1 teaspoon of cornstarch. Stir well and set aside.

2 Combine the egg white, salt, 2 tablespoons of the oil, and the remaining cornstarch. Toss and coat the chicken in the mixture.

3 In a wok or skillet, heat the remaining oil until hot. Add the chicken in batches and stir-fry until golden. Remove from the wok, drain on paper towels, and set aside to keep warm.

4 Add more oil to the wok, if needed, and stir-fry the mushrooms, then add the broccoli and cook for 2–3 minutes.

5 Return the chicken to the wok and add the bean sprouts, water chestnuts, and pistachio nuts. Stir-fry until all the ingredients are thoroughly warm. Add the chicken stock mixture and cook, stirring continuously, until thickened.

6 Serve immediately over a bed of freshly cooked rice, garnished with pistachios.

52

Spice Chicken with Zucchini

SERVES 4

1 tablespoon peanut oil
   or vegetable oil

1 clove garlic, finely chopped

1-inch piece fresh ginger,
   finely chopped

1 small fresh red chile, seeded and
   finely chopped

12 ounces skinless, boneless chicken
   breasts, cut into thin strips

1 tablespoon five-spice powder

1 red bell pepper, seeded and sliced

1 yellow bell pepper, seeded
   and sliced

2 zucchini, thinly sliced

8-ounce can bamboo shoots, drained

2 tablespoons dry sherry or
   apple juice

1 tablespoon light soy sauce

2 tablespoons chopped fresh
   cilantro, plus extra to garnish

salt and pepper

Method

1 Heat the oil in a wok or large skillet. Add the garlic, ginger, and chile and stir-fry for 30 seconds to release the flavors.

2 Add the chicken and five-spice powder and stir-fry for about 4 minutes, or until the chicken has colored all over. Add the red bell pepper, yellow bell pepper, and zucchini and stir-fry for 1–2 minutes, or until slightly soft.

3 Stir in the bamboo shoots and stir-fry for another 2–3 minutes, or until the chicken is cooked through and tender. Add the sherry and soy sauce, season with salt and pepper, and let sizzle for 1–2 minutes.

4 Stir in the cilantro and serve immediately, garnished with extra cilantro.

53

Chicken Fried Rice

SERVES 4

1/2 tablespoon sesame oil

6 shallots, peeled and quartered

3 cups cooked, cubed chicken

3 tablespoons soy sauce

2 carrots, diced

1 celery stalk, diced

1 red bell pepper, seeded and diced

1 1/4 cups fresh peas

2/3 cup of canned corn kernels

2 cups leftover, cooked
   long-grain rice

2 extra-large eggs, scrambled

Method

1 Heat the oil in a large wok or skillet over medium heat. Add the shallots and cook until soft, then add the chicken and 2 tablespoons of the soy sauce and stir-fry for 5–6 minutes.

2 Stir in the carrots, celery, red bell pepper, peas, and corn and stir-fry for another 5 minutes. Add the rice and stir thoroughly.

3 Finally, stir in the scrambled eggs and the remaining soy sauce. Serve immediately.

54

Ginger Chicken with Noodles

SERVES 4

2 tablespoons peanut oil or
vegetable oil

1 onion, sliced

2 garlic cloves, finely chopped

2-inch piece fresh ginger, thinly
sliced

2 carrots, thinly sliced

4 skinless, boneless chicken breasts,
cut into cubes

1¼ cups chicken stock

¼ cup Thai soy sauce

8-ounce can bamboo shoots,
drained and rinsed

3 ounces flat rice noodles

4 chopped scallions and
¼ cup chopped fresh cilantro,
to garnish

Method

1 Heat the oil in a wok and stir-fry the onion, garlic, ginger, and carrots for 1–2 minutes, until soft. Add the chicken and stir-fry for 3–4 minutes, until the chicken is cooked through and lightly browned.

2 Add the stock, soy sauce, and bamboo shoots and gradually bring to a boil. Simmer for 2–3 minutes.

3 Meanwhile, bring a saucepan of water to a boil, add the noodles, and soak for 6–8 minutes, or cook according to the package directions. Drain well, then garnish with the scallions and cilantro. Serve immediately with the chicken stir-fry.

55

Turkey Teriyaki

SERVES 4

1 pound turkey cutlets,
  cut into strips

3 tablespoons peanut oil
  or vegetable oil

1 small yellow bell pepper, seeded
  and sliced into thin strips

8 scallions, green part included,
  diagonally sliced into
  1-inch pieces

freshly cooked, plain rice, to serve

Teriyaki glaze

1/3 cup shoyu (Japanese soy sauce)

1/3 cup mirin

2 tablespoons honey

1 teaspoon finely chopped
  fresh ginger

Method

1 Mix the glaze ingredients in a small saucepan over low–medium heat. Stir until the honey has melted, then remove from the heat and let cool.

2 Put the turkey in a large, shallow dish. Pour over the glaze, turning the strips so they are well coated. Let marinate for 30 minutes at room temperature, or overnight in the refrigerator.

3 Using a slotted spoon, remove the turkey from the marinade, shaking off the excess liquid. Reserve the marinade.

4 Heat a wok over medium–high heat, then add the oil. Add the turkey and stir-fry for 2 minutes. Add the yellow bell pepper and scallions and cook for 1 minute. Pour in the reserved marinade. Bring to a boil, then reduce the heat slightly and cook for 3–4 minutes, until the turkey is cooked through.

5 Transfer the turkey and vegetables to a warm serving dish. Boil the liquid remaining in the wok until syrupy, then pour over the turkey. Serve immediately with rice.

56

Turkey with Bok Choy

SERVES 4

8 ounces medium egg noodles

3 tablespoons peanut oil
or vegetable oil

1 large garlic clove, thinly sliced

2 teaspoons finely chopped
fresh ginger

1 pound turkey cutlets,
cut into thin strips

3 cups thinly sliced cremini
mushrooms

1 small head bok choy, stems cut
into 1-inch pieces and leaves
sliced into wide ribbons

4 scallions, green part included,
diagonally sliced into
1-inch pieces

1 tablespoon light soy sauce

2 tablespoons chopped fresh cilantro

salt and pepper

Method

1 Cook the noodles in a saucepan of boiling water for
4 minutes, or according to the package directions,
until soft. Drain, rinse, and drain again, then let cool.

2 Heat a wok over medium–high heat, then add the oil.
Stir-fry the garlic and ginger for a few seconds to flavor
the oil.

3 Add the turkey and stir-fry for 2 minutes, until no longer
pink. Add the mushrooms and bok choy stems, and stir-fry
for 2 minutes. Add the bok choy leaves and scallions, and
stir-fry for another 2 minutes. Stir in the noodles and soy
sauce, and season with salt and pepper. Cook until the noodles
are heated through, then add the cilantro. Serve immediately.

57

Turkey with Hoisin Sauce

SERVES 4

1 pound turkey cutlets, cubed

4 tablespoons peanut oil
 or vegetable oil

3 large garlic cloves, thinly sliced

4 scallions, white and green parts
 separated, diagonally sliced into
 ¾-inch pieces

1 tablespoon Chinese rice wine
 or dry sherry

3 tablespoons hoisin sauce

¼ cup cashew nuts

Marinade

1 teaspoon cornstarch

1 tablespoon Chinese rice wine
 or dry sherry

¼ teaspoon white pepper

½ teaspoon salt

½ egg white, lightly beaten

2 teaspoons sesame oil

Method

1 To make the marinade, mix the cornstarch and rice wine to a paste. Add the pepper, salt, egg white, and sesame oil, mixing well. Put the turkey in a shallow dish and add the marinade, turning to coat. Let stand for 30 minutes.

2 Heat a wok over high heat, then add 3 tablespoons of the peanut oil. Add the garlic and white scallions, and stir for a few seconds to flavor the oil. Add the turkey and reduce the heat slightly. Stir-fry for 2 minutes, until no longer pink, then sprinkle with the rice wine. Transfer to a plate with a slotted spoon.

3 Increase the heat to high and add the remaining peanut oil. Swirl the oil around the wok, then stir in the hoisin sauce. Return the turkey mixture to the wok and stir-fry for 2–3 minutes, turning to coat, until cooked through.

4 Add the cashew nuts and green scallion. Transfer to a warm serving dish and serve immediately.

58

Lemon Turkey with Spinach

SERVES 4

1 pound turkey cutlets,
   cut into strips

1 tablespoon vegetable oil

6 scallions, finely sliced

1/2 lemon, peeled and thinly sliced

1 garlic clove, finely chopped

10 ounces spinach, washed, drained,
   and coarsely chopped

1/4 cup chopped fresh
   flat-leaf parsley

sprigs of flat-leaf parsley and
   lemon slices, to garnish

cooked pasta, to serve

Marinade

1 tablespoon soy sauce

1 tablespoon white wine vinegar

1 teaspoon cornstarch

1 teaspoon finely grated lemon zest

1/2 teaspoon pepper

Method

1 To make the marinade, put the soy sauce, vinegar, cornstarch, lemon zest, and pepper in a bowl and mix thoroughly. Add the turkey and stir to coat. Cover with plastic wrap and marinate in the refrigerator for 30 minutes.

2 Heat the oil in a large wok or skillet. Add the turkey and the marinade and cook over medium heat for 2–3 minutes, or until the turkey is opaque.

3 Add the scallions, lemon slices, and garlic and cook for another 2–3 minutes. Stir in the spinach and parsley and cook until the spinach is just wilted.

4 Remove from the heat, spoon over freshly cooked pasta, and garnish with sprigs of parsley and lemon slices before serving.

59

Duck with Mixed Bell Peppers

SERVES 4

1 tablespoon peanut oil
   or vegetable oil

2 boneless duck breasts, skin on,
   weighing about 1¼ pounds
   in total

1 onion, sliced

2 garlic cloves, chopped

1 red bell pepper, seeded and sliced

1 green bell pepper, seeded
   and sliced

1 yellow bell pepper, seeded
   and sliced

4 tomatoes, peeled, seeded,
   and chopped

2/3 cup stock

3 tablespoons Thai soy sauce

freshly cooked noodles sprinkled
   with scallions, to serve

Method

1 Heat a wok over high heat, then add the oil. Cook
the duck, skin-side down, for 5–10 minutes, or until crisp
and brown. Turn over and cook for another 5 minutes,
until cooked through. Remove the duck from the wok and
keep warm.

2 Pour off any excess fat and stir-fry the onion and garlic
for 2–3 minutes, until softened and lightly browned.

3 Add the bell peppers and stir-fry for 2–3 minutes, until
tender. Add the tomatoes, stock, and soy sauce, and simmer
for 1–2 minutes. Transfer to a serving plate. Slice the duck
thickly and arrange on top, spooning any sauce over it.
Serve with noodles.

60

Cantonese Sweet & Sour Duck

SERVES 4

2 boneless duck breasts, skin on, weighing about 1¼ pounds in total

½ tablespoon soy sauce

2 teaspoons peanut oil or vegetable oil

salt and pepper

1½-inch piece cucumber, peeled and sliced lengthwise into matchsticks, to garnish

Sauce

1 tablespoon cornstarch

½ cup chicken stock

1½ tablespoons soy sauce

1½ tablespoons rice vinegar

2 tablespoons sugar

1 tablespoon tomato paste

1 tablespoon orange juice

2 teaspoons peanut oil or vegetable oil

3 thin slices fresh ginger

Method

1 Slice each duck breast into three pieces and put in a dish. Rub with salt and pepper and the ½ tablespoon of soy sauce.

2 Heat a wok over medium–high heat, then add the oil. Cook the duck for 6 minutes, starting with the skin-side down, and turning until brown and crisp on all sides. Using tongs, transfer to a plate and let rest in a warm place for 10 minutes. Discard the oil and wipe the wok clean with paper towels. Slice the duck into ½-inch strips (the meat will still be rare at this stage).

3 To prepare the sauce, mix the cornstarch to a smooth paste with 3 tablespoons of the stock. Combine the soy sauce, vinegar, and sugar in a small bowl, stirring to dissolve the sugar. Add the tomato paste and orange juice, mixing well.

4 Heat the oil in the clean wok over medium heat. Add the ginger slices and stir-fry for a few seconds to flavor the oil. Add the soy sauce mixture and the remaining stock and bring to a boil. Reduce the heat slightly and add in the cornstarch paste. Stir until starting to thicken, then add the duck slices, stirring to coat with the sauce. Simmer over low heat for 5 minutes, until the duck is cooked but still slightly pink.

5 Remove the ginger slices and transfer the duck and sauce to a warm serving dish. Garnish with the cucumber and serve immediately.

61

Duck with Black Beans

SERVES 2–3

2 small duck breasts, weighing
   1 pound in total

2 tablespoons salted black beans

1 1/2 tablespoons soy sauce

1 tablespoon rice vinegar

2 teaspoons sugar

1/3 head broccoli

3 tablespoons peanut oil
   or vegetable oil

1-inch piece fresh ginger,
   cut into thin shreds

1 fresh red chile, seeded and thinly
   sliced diagonally

1 large garlic clove, thinly sliced

1/2 red bell pepper, seeded
   and thinly sliced

Method

1 Remove and discard the skin from the duck. Slice the meat into 1/4-inch strips.

2 Soak the beans in cold water for 30 minutes, then drain. Combine the soy sauce, vinegar, and sugar in a small bowl, stirring to dissolve the sugar.

3 Divide the broccoli into florets. Slice the stems thinly and slice the florets into pieces no more than 3/4 inch wide.

4 Heat a wok over medium heat, then add the oil. Heat the ginger, chile, and garlic for a few seconds to flavor the oil. Add the drained beans, broccoli, and red bell pepper. Increase the heat to high and stir-fry for 2 minutes.

5 Add the duck and stir-fry for 2 minutes, then add the soy sauce mixture. Continue to stir-fry for another 2 minutes. Serve immediately.

62

Three-Pea Stir-Fry with Duck

SERVES 4

2 small skinless, boneless duck
    breasts, weighing about
    1 pound in total

3 tablespoons peanut oil
    or vegetable oil

6 large scallions, white and green
    parts separated, diagonally sliced
    into 3/4-inch pieces

1 teaspoon finely chopped fresh
    ginger

3 cups sugar snap peas

2 cups snow peas, diagonally halved

1 cup shelled peas

1/4 cup whole almonds with skin,
    halved lengthwise

1/2 cup fresh bean sprouts

freshly cooked noodles, to serve

Marinade

1 tablespoon light brown sugar

3 tablespoons warm water

1–2 fresh red chiles, seeded and
    finely chopped

1 tablespoon soy sauce

1 teaspoon Thai fish sauce

3 tablespoons lime juice

Method

1 Combine the marinade ingredients in a bowl, stirring to dissolve the sugar. Slice the duck into bite-size pieces and add to the marinade. Let stand at room temperature for 30 minutes, or overnight in the refrigerator.

2 Heat a wok over high heat, then add the oil. Stir-fry the white scallion and the ginger for a few seconds. Add the duck and the marinade, and stir-fry for about 5 minutes. When the liquid has reduced slightly, add the three types of peas and stir-fry for another 2–3 minutes.

3 Add the almonds, bean sprouts, and green scallion, and stir-fry for a few seconds to heat through. Serve with noodles.

4

FISH & SEAFOOD

63

Thai Green Fish Curry

SERVES 4

2 tablespoons vegetable oil

1 garlic clove, chopped

2 tablespoons Thai green curry paste

1 small eggplant, diced

1/2 cup coconut milk

2 tablespoons Thai fish sauce

1 teaspoon sugar

8 ounces firm white fish fillets, such as cod, halibut, or red snapper, cut into pieces

1/2 cup fish stock

2 kaffir lime leaves, finely shredded

about 15 fresh Thai basil leaves

sprigs of fresh dill, to garnish

Method

1 Heat the vegetable oil in a large skillet or preheated wok over medium heat until almost smoking. Add the garlic and cook until golden. Add the curry paste and stir-fry a few seconds before adding the eggplant. Stir-fry for about 4–5 minutes, until softened.

2 Add the coconut milk, bring to a boil, and stir until it thickens and curdles slightly. Add the fish sauce and sugar to the skillet and stir well.

3 Add the fish pieces and stock. Simmer for 3–4 minutes, stirring occasionally, until the fish is just tender. Add the lime leaves and basil, then cook for another 1 minute. Transfer to a warm serving dish and garnish with a few sprigs of fresh dill. Serve immediately.

64

Fried Fish with Pine Nuts

SERVES 4–6

1/2 teaspoon salt

1 pound thick white fish fillets, such as cod, halibut, or red snapper, cut into 1-inch cubes

2 dried Chinese mushrooms, soaked in warm water for 20 minutes

3 tablespoons peanut oil or vegetable oil

1-inch piece of fresh ginger, finely shredded

1 tablespoon chopped scallion

1 red bell pepper, cut into 1-inch squares

1 green bell pepper, cut into 1-inch squares

1/4 cup rinsed and cubed fresh or canned bamboo shoots (if using fresh shoots, first boil in water for 30 minutes)

2 teaspoons Chinese rice wine or dry sherry

2 tablespoons pine nuts, toasted

cooked rice, to serve

Method

1 Sprinkle the salt over the fish and set aside for 20 minutes. Squeeze out any excess water from the mushrooms and slice finely, discarding any tough stems.

2 In a preheated wok, heat 2 tablespoons of the oil and cook the fish for 3 minutes. Drain the fish, set aside, and then wipe the wok clean.

3 Preheat the clean wok, heat the remaining oil, and toss in the ginger. Stir until fragrant, then add the scallion, bell peppers, bamboo shoots, mushrooms, and rice wine and cook for 1–2 minutes.

4 Finally, add the fish and stir to warm through. Sprinkle with pine nuts and serve with freshly cooked rice.

65

Rice Noodles with Fried Fish

SERVES 6

8 ounces dried fine rice noodles

1/2 cup rice flour or all-purpose flour

1/2 teaspoon ground turmeric

2 pounds white fish fillets, such as tilapia or flounder, cut into 3/4-inch cubes

2 tablespoons peanut oil or vegetable oil, plus extra for deep-frying

4 scallions, cut into 1-inch lengths

1/3 cup dry-roasted, unsalted peanuts

24 fresh Thai basil leaves

24 fresh dill sprigs, trimmed

24 fresh cilantro sprigs, trimmed

salt and pepper

Method

1 Cook the noodles according to the package directions, until tender. Transfer to individual serving dishes.

2 Put the flour and turmeric in a sealable plastic food bag and season with salt and pepper. Shake to mix well. Add the fish cubes, then seal the bag and shake to coat each fish cube evenly.

3 Heat enough oil for deep-frying in a wok to 350–375°F, or until a cube of bread browns in 30 seconds. Working in small batches, take a handful of fish cubes and shake off the excess flour, then lower into the hot oil. Deep-fry for 2–3 minutes, or until golden and crisp. Drain on paper towels. Divide the fried fish cubes equally among the serving dishes.

4 Heat a clean wok over high heat, then add the 2 tablespoons of oil. Add the scallions and peanuts and stir-fry for 1 minute. Add the basil, dill, and cilantro and stir-fry for 1–2 minutes, or until just wilted. Divide among the serving dishes and serve immediately.

66

Cod with Spiced Noodles

SERVES 4

2 tablespoons peanut oil or
vegetable oil, plus extra
for brushing

juice and finely grated rind of
1 large lemon

4 cod, halibut, or haddock steaks,
about 5 ounces each, skinned

paprika, to taste

salt and pepper

Spiced noodles

8 ounces dried medium egg noodles

2 garlic cloves, chopped

1-inch piece fresh ginger, finely
chopped

2 tablespoons finely chopped
fresh coriander root or 1/4 cup
cilantro stems

1 tablespoon kecap manis
(sweet soy sauce)

1 fresh red Thai chile, seeded and
finely chopped

1 tablespoon Thai fish sauce

Method

1 Preheat the broiler to high. Put the noodles in a saucepan of boiling water and cook for 3 minutes, or cook according to the package directions, until tender. Drain, rinse with cold water, and drain again, then set aside.

2 Mix 1 tablespoon of the oil with the lemon juice and brush over one side of each fish steak. Sprinkle with the lemon rind and paprika and season with salt and pepper. Lightly brush a broiler rack with oil, then place the fish on the rack and cook under the preheated broiler for 8–10 minutes, until the flesh flakes easily.

3 Meanwhile, heat a wok over high heat, then add the remaining oil. Add the garlic and ginger and stir-fry for about 30 seconds. Add the coriander root and kecap manis and stir. Add the noodles and stir thoroughly so they are coated in the kecap manis. Stir in the chile and fish sauce. Divide the spiced noodles among individual serving plates, top each with a fish steak, and serve immediately.

67

Fish with Tomatoes & Herbs

SERVES 6

1 1/4 cups all-purpose flour

6 flounder or tilapia fillets,
    about 6 ounces each

1/4–1/3 cup peanut oil or vegetable oil

2 large garlic cloves, thinly sliced

4 ripe tomatoes, quartered

1 tablespoon Thai fish sauce

12 fresh dill sprigs, trimmed

12 fresh cilantro sprigs, trimmed

12 fresh Thai basil leaves

salt and pepper

rice and sweet-and-sour fish sauce,
    to serve

Method

1 Put the flour in a sealable plastic food bag and season with salt and pepper. Add the fish. Seal the bag and toss the fish gently to coat with flour.

2 Heat 2 tablespoons of oil in a skillet over high heat. Working in batches and adding extra oil as needed, cook the fish fillets for 5–7 minutes, or until golden and crisp on both sides. Transfer to a serving plate.

3 Heat a wok over high heat, then add 1 tablespoon of oil. Add the garlic and stir-fry for 3–5 minutes, or until just golden. Add the tomatoes and fish sauce and stir-fry for 10 minutes, or until softened. Adjust the seasoning, adding salt and pepper if needed. Spoon the tomato mixture on top of the fish.

4 Wipe out the wok with paper towels, then heat 1 tablespoon of oil over high heat. Add the dill, cilantro, and basil and stir-fry for 1–2 minutes, or until just wilted. Scatter the herbs over the tomatoes and fish. Serve with rice and sweet-and-sour fish sauce.

68

Shrimp Fu Yung

SERVES 4–6

1 tablespoon peanut oil
  or vegetable oil

4 ounces large shrimp, peeled and
  deveined

4 eggs, lightly beaten

1 teaspoon salt

pinch of white pepper

2 tablespoons finely chopped
  Chinese chives, garlic shoots,
  or regular chives

Method

1 Heat a wok over high heat and add the oil. Add the shrimp and stir-fry for about 4 minutes, or until just pink.

2 Season the eggs with the salt and pepper and pour over the shrimp. Stir-fry for 1 minute, then add the chives.

3 Cook for another 4 minutes, stirring all the time, until the eggs are cooked through but still soft in texture. Serve immediately.

69

Steamed Salmon with Asparagus

SERVES 4

4 salmon steaks, about
   1 inch thick

2 teaspoon finely chopped
   fresh ginger

2 tablespoons Chinese rice wine
   or dry sherry

1 tablespoon light soy sauce

1/2 teaspoon salt

8 asparagus spears

4 tablespoons peanut oil

3 heads bok choy,
   quartered lengthwise

good squeeze of lime juice

2 teaspoon sesame oil

pepper

freshly cooked, plain rice, to serve

Method

1 Place the salmon steaks in a single layer on a heatproof plate that will fit into a wok. Combine the ginger, wine, soy sauce, and salt. Sprinkle this over the fish, rubbing it into the flesh, and let stand for 20 minutes, turning once.

2 Snap the woody ends from the asparagus and discard. Cut off the tips and reserve. Chop the stems into two or three pieces.

3 Place a trivet in a wok with a lid, and add enough water to come halfway up the trivet. Bring to a boil, then place the plate of fish on the trivet and cover with a loose tent of aluminum foil. Adjust the heat so the water is only just boiling. Put the lid on the wok and steam for 10–15 minutes, until the fish is opaque and just starting to flake.

4 Meanwhile, heat a second wok over high heat, then add 2 tablespoons of the peanut oil. Add the asparagus stalks and bok choy, and stir-fry for 4–5 minutes until just tender but still crisp. Splash with a good squeeze of lime juice and season with salt and pepper. Arrange in small mounds on warm serving plates.

5 Carefully lift the salmon steaks from the wok and place on top of the vegetables. Heat the sesame oil and remaining peanut oil until hot. Add the asparagus tips and stir-fry for 20 seconds, until barely cooked. Season with pepper. Arrange the tips on top of the fish and pour the hot oil over the top. Serve immediately with rice.

70

Stir-Fried Salmon with Leeks

SERVES 4

1 pound salmon fillet, skinned

2 tablespoons kecap manis
(sweet soy sauce)

2 tablespoons ketchup

1 teaspoon rice vinegar

1 tablespoon demerara sugar or
other raw sugar

1 garlic clove, crushed

4 tablespoons peanut oil
or vegetable oil

5 leeks, thinly shredded

sliced fresh red chiles, to garnish

Method

1 Using a sharp knife, cut the salmon into slices. Place the slices of salmon in a shallow, nonmetallic dish.

2 Mix the kecap manis, ketchup, vinegar, sugar, and garlic together in a small bowl. Pour the mixture over the salmon, toss well, and let marinate for about 30 minutes.

3 Meanwhile, heat a wok over medium–high heat, then add 3 tablespoons of the oil. Add the leeks to the wok and stir-fry for about 10 minutes, or until the leeks become crispy and tender.

4 Using a slotted spoon, carefully remove the leeks from the wok and transfer to warm serving plates.

5 Add the remaining oil to the wok. Add the salmon and the marinade to the wok and cook for 2 minutes. Remove the salmon from the wok, spoon over the leeks, garnish with chiles, and serve immediately.

71

Teriyaki Tuna with Vegetables

SERVES 4

4 tuna steaks, about 4 ounces each,
   cut into strips

8 ounces dried medium egg noodles

1 tablespoon toasted sesame seeds
   and 2 scallions, diagonally sliced,
   to garnish

Marinade

1/2 cup teriyaki sauce

2 teaspoons honey

salt and pepper

Stir-fry

1 tablespoon vegetable oil

2 teaspoons sesame oil

1 carrot, cut into thin strips

2 heads bok choy, stems and leaves
   separated and finely sliced

1 yellow bell pepper, seeded and
   cut into thin strips

2 garlic cloves, chopped

1 tablespoon soy sauce

Method

1 For the marinade, mix together the teriyaki sauce, honey, and salt and pepper to taste in a shallow dish. Add the tuna and turn to coat in the marinade. Cover with plastic wrap and let marinate in the refrigerator for 1 hour, turning the tuna occasionally.

2 Cook the noodles according to the package directions, until tender. Drain well and set aside.

3 Meanwhile, preheat the broiler to high. Line the broiler pan with aluminum foil. Remove the tuna from the marinade, reserving the marinade, and arrange in the broiler pan. Spoon over half of the marinade and cook under the preheated broiler for 1 minute. Turn over, spoon over the remaining marinade, and cook for another minute.

4 Heat a wok over high heat, then add the oils. Stir-fry the carrot, bok choy stalks, and yellow bell pepper for 2 minutes. Add the garlic and bok choy leaves and stir-fry for 1 minute. Add the soy sauce and a little water. Divide the noodles among four individual serving bowls. Top with the stir-fried vegetables, tuna, and any cooking juices, and garnish with the sesame seeds and scallions.

72

Seafood Chow Mein

SERVES 4

3 ounces squid, cleaned

3–4 fresh scallops

3 ounces shrimp, peeled
and deveined

1/2 egg white, lightly beaten

2 teaspoons cornstarch, mixed to a
paste with 2 1/2 teaspoons water

10 ounces dried fine egg noodles

5–6 tablespoons vegetable oil

2 tablespoons light soy sauce

1 cup snow peas, sliced diagonally

1/2 teaspoon salt

1/2 teaspoon sugar

1 teaspoon Chinese rice wine
or dry sherry

2 scallions, finely shredded

a few drops of sesame oil

Method

1 Open up the squid and score the inside in a crisscross pattern,
then cut into pieces about 1 inch square. Soak the squid in a
bowl of boiling water until all the pieces curl up. Rinse in cold
water and drain.

2 Cut each scallop into 3–4 slices. Cut the shrimp in half
lengthwise if large. Mix the scallops and shrimp with the egg
white and cornstarch.

3 Cook the noodles according to the package directions, then
drain and rinse under cold water. Drain well, then toss with about
1 tablespoon of the oil.

4 Heat 3 tablespoons of the oil in a preheated wok. Add the
noodles and 1 tablespoon of the soy sauce and stir-fry for
2–3 minutes. Remove to a large serving dish.

5 Heat the remaining oil in the wok and add the snow peas and
seafood. Stir-fry for about 2 minutes, then add the salt, sugar, rice
wine, the remaining soy sauce, and about half of the scallions.
Blend well and add a little water if necessary. Pour the seafood
mixture on top of the noodles and sprinkle with sesame oil.
Garnish with the remaining scallions and serve immediately.

73

Seafood Curry

SERVES 4

1 tablespoon oil peanut or
    vegetable oil

3 shallots, finely chopped

1-inch piece fresh galangal or ginger,
    peeled and thinly sliced

2 garlic cloves, finely chopped

14-ounce can coconut milk

2 lemongrass stalks, snapped in half

1/4 cup Thai fish sauce

2 tablespoons chili sauce

8 ounces jumbo shrimp,
    peeled and deveined

8 ounces baby squid, cleaned
    and thickly sliced

8 ounces salmon fillet, skinned
    and cut into chunks

6 ounces tuna steak, cut into chunks

8 ounces fresh mussels, scrubbed
    and debearded

lime wedges, to garnish

cooked jasmine rice, to serve

Method

1 Heat a wok over medium–high heat, then add the oil. Add the shallots, galangal, and garlic and stir-fry for about 2 minutes, until they start to soften. Add the coconut milk, lemongrass, fish sauce, and chili sauce. Bring to a boil, reduce the heat, and simmer for 1–2 minutes.

2 Add the shrimp, squid, salmon, and tuna and simmer for 3–4 minutes, until the shrimp have turned pink and the fish is cooked.

3 Discard any mussels with broken shells or any that refuse to close when tapped. Add the remaining mussels to the wok and cover with a lid. Simmer for 1–2 minutes, until they have opened. Discard any mussels that remain closed. Garnish with lime wedges and serve immediately with rice.

74

Quick Seafood Rice

SERVES 4

2 tablespoons peanut oil
or vegetable oil

1 large onion, chopped

1 garlic clove, finely chopped

8 large tomatoes, peeled, seeded,
and chopped

1 1/4 cups paella or risotto rice

about 3 1/2 cups fish stock

1 pound mussels, scrubbed
and debearded

14 ounces frozen mixed seafood,
such as cod, tilapia, and shrimp,
thawed

1 1/4 cups young green peas,
thawed if frozen

2 tablespoons chopped fresh parsley,
plus extra to garnish

salt and pepper

Method

1 Heat a wok over high heat, then add the oil. Add the onion and cook until just softened. Add the garlic and half of the tomatoes and stir together well. Add the rice and stir-fry for 2–3 minutes, then add half of the stock and bring to a boil. Simmer for 12–15 minutes, adding more stock as necessary.

2 Discard any mussels with broken shells and any that refuse to close when tapped. Add the remaining mussels to the wok with the mixed seafood and peas. Season with salt and pepper and cook for another 3–4 minutes, until hot, the mussels have opened, and the liquid has been mostly absorbed. Discard any mussels that remain closed.

3 Stir in the remaining tomatoes and the parsley. Taste and adjust the seasoning, adding salt and pepper if needed. Serve immediately, garnished with extra parsley.

75

Teriyaki Shrimp

SERVES 4

1½ tablespoons peanut oil
    or vegetable oil

2½ cups snow peas

10 ears of baby corn

1 large orange or yellow bell pepper,
    seeded and thinly sliced

8 scallions, halved lengthwise

2 garlic cloves, well crushed

¾-inch piece fresh ginger,
    peeled and finely chopped

2 tablespoons teriyaki marinade

1 cup cashew nuts

1 pound large cooked, peeled shrimp

1 tablespoon sesame oil

Method

1 Heat the peanut oil in a large, preheated wok or skillet, add all the vegetables, and stir-fry over high heat for 4 minutes, or until almost tender. Add the garlic and ginger and stir-fry for 1 minute.

2 Add the teriyaki marinade, cashew nuts, and shrimp and stir-fry for 2 minutes.

3 Serve immediately, with the sesame oil drizzled over.

76

Shrimp Noodle Bowl

SERVES 4

1 bunch scallions

2 celery stalks

1 red bell pepper

8 ounces vermicelli rice noodles

2 tablespoons peanut oil
  or vegetable oil

1/3 cup unsalted peanuts

1 fresh Thai chile, sliced

1 lemongrass stem, crushed

13/4 cups fish stock or chicken stock

1 cup coconut milk

2 teaspoons Thai fish sauce

12 ounces cooked, peeled
  jumbo shrimp

salt and pepper

3 tablespoons chopped fresh
  cilantro, to garnish

Method

1 Trim the scallions and celery and thinly slice diagonally. Seed and thinly slice the red bell pepper.

2 Place the noodles in a bowl, cover with boiling water, and let stand for 4 minutes, or according to package directions, until tender. Drain.

3 Heat the oil in a wok, add the peanuts, and stir-fry for 1–2 minutes, until golden. Lift out with a slotted spoon. Add the sliced vegetables to the wok and stir-fry over high heat for 1–2 minutes. Add the chile, lemongrass, stock, coconut milk, and fish sauce and bring to a boil.

4 Stir in the shrimp and bring back to a boil, stirring. Season with salt and pepper, then add the noodles. Serve in warm bowls, sprinkled with fresh cilantro.

77

Sesame Noodles with Shrimp

SERVES 2

1 tablespoon oil

16 shrimp, peeled and deveined

3 shiitake mushrooms, finely sliced

1/4 head green cabbage, shredded

1 carrot, grated

2 bundles of somen noodles

6 shiso leaves, shredded

Dressing

3 tablespoons vegetable oil

1 tablespoon sesame seeds, toasted

1/2 cup Japanese rice vinegar

1 tablespoon sugar

1 tablespoon usukuchi shoyu
(Japanese light soy sauce)

salt, to taste

Method

1 To make the dressing, mix and all the ingredients together in a nonmetallic bowl.

2 Heat the oil in a wok. Add the shrimp and cook until pink.

3 Add the mushrooms and stir-fry for 1 minute, then add the cabbage and carrot. Remove from the heat and let cool.

4 Cook the noodles according to the package directions, then drain.

5 Put the noodles in a bowl, add the shrimp mixture and dressing, and mix well.

6 Sprinkle with the shiso leaves and serve.

78

Scallop Stir-Fry

SERVES 4

1 teaspoon peanut oil
or vegetable oil

2-inch piece fresh ginger, grated

1 tablespoon finely grated lime rind

1 orange bell pepper, seeded
and sliced

1 red onion, thinly sliced

10 ounces scallops

4 ounces wild mushrooms,
such as chanterelle, or
cremini mushrooms

1/4 cup lime juice

1 teaspoon honey (optional)

1 tablespoon soy sauce

1 1/2 cups shredded bok choy

Method

1 Heat a wok over high heat, then add the oil. Add the ginger and cook, stirring, for 1 minute.

2 Add the lime rind, bell pepper, and onion and stir-fry for 3–4 minutes, or until the onion has softened. Add the scallops and mushrooms to the wok and stir-fry for 2 minutes.

3 Pour in the lime juice, add the honey, if using, and the soy sauce. Stir together, then add the bok choy and continue to cook for 2–3 minutes, or until the scallops are tender. Serve immediately.

79

Scallop & Snow Peas Stir-Fry

SERVES 4

3 tablespoons peanut oil
  or vegetable oil

2 tablespoons sesame oil

16 large scallops, halved

8 ounces small shiitake mushrooms,
  tough stems removed

3 cups snow peas, trimmed and
  halved diagonally

2 teaspoons finely chopped fresh
  ginger

2 garlic cloves, finely chopped

2 teaspoons light soy sauce

juice of 1 lime

1/4 cup torn cilantro leaves

salt and pepper

Method

1 Heat a wok over high heat and add the oils. Stir-fry the scallops for 1 minute. Add the mushrooms and snow peas and stir-fry for another minute.

2 Add the ginger, garlic, soy sauce, and a splash of water to moisten. Stir-fry for another 1–2 minutes, until the vegetables are just tender.

3 Add the lime juice and cilantro leaves, and season with salt and pepper. Divide among plates and serve immediately.

80

Stir-Fried Crab with Ginger

SERVES 4

3 tablespoons peanut oil
   or vegetable oil

2 large fresh crabs, such as blue
   crabs or Dungeness crabs, cleaned,
   broken into pieces, and legs
   cracked with a cleaver

1½-inch piece fresh ginger, cut into
   julienne strips

6 scallions, chopped into
   2-inch lengths

2 tablespoons light soy sauce

1 teaspoon sugar

pinch of white pepper

Method

1 Heat a wok over high heat, then add 2 tablespoons of the oil. Stir-fry the crab for 3–4 minutes. Remove from the wok and set aside.

2 Heat the remaining oil in the wok, add the ginger and stir until fragrant. Add the scallions, then stir in the crab pieces. Add the soy sauce, sugar, and pepper. Cover and simmer for 1 minute. Serve immediately.

81

Clams in Black Bean Sauce

SERVES 4

2 pounds small clams

1 tablespoon peanut oil
   or vegetable oil

1 teaspoon finely chopped
   fresh ginger

1 teaspoon finely chopped garlic

1 tablespoon fermented black beans,
   rinsed and coarsely chopped

2 teaspoons Chinese rice wine
   or dry sherry

1 tablespoons finely chopped
   scallion

1 teaspoon salt (optional)

Method

1 Discard any clams with broken shells and any that refuse to close when tapped. Wash the remaining clams thoroughly and let soak in clean water until ready to cook.

2 In a preheated wok or large skillet, heat the oil and stir-fry the ginger and garlic until fragrant. Add the black beans and cook for 1 minute.

3 Over high heat, add the clams and rice wine and stir-fry for 2 minutes to mix everything together. Cover and cook for an additional 3 minutes. Add the scallion and salt, if necessary, and serve immediately.

82

Squid with Black Bean Sauce

SERVES 4

1¾ pounds squid, cleaned and
tentacles discarded

1 large red bell pepper, seeded

2 cups snow peas

1 head bok choy

1½ tablespoons vegetable oil

1 small fresh red Thai chile, chopped

1 garlic clove, finely chopped

1 teaspoon grated fresh ginger

2 scallions, chopped

Sauce

3 tablespoons black bean sauce

1 tablespoon Thai fish sauce

1 tablespoon rice wine or dry sherry

1 tablespoon dark soy sauce

1 teaspoon brown sugar

1 teaspoon cornstarch

1 tablespoon water

Method

1 Cut the squid body cavities into quarters lengthwise. Use the tip of a small, sharp knife to score a diamond pattern into the flesh without cutting all the way through. Pat dry with paper towels.

2 Cut the bell pepper into long, thin slices. Cut the snow peas in half diagonally. Coarsely shred the bok choy.

3 To make the sauce, mix the black bean sauce, fish sauce, rice wine, soy sauce, and sugar together in a bowl. Blend the cornstarch with the water and stir into the other ingredients in the bowl. Reserve the mixture until required.

4 Heat the oil in a preheated wok. Add the chile, garlic, ginger, and scallions and stir-fry for 1 minute. Add the bell pepper slices and stir-fry for 2 minutes.

5 Add the squid and stir-fry over high heat for 1 minute. Stir in the snow peas and bok choy and stir for another 1 minute, or until wilted.

6 Stir in the sauce and cook, stirring continuously, for 2 minutes, or until the sauce thickens and clears. Serve immediately.

5

VEGETABLES

83

Red Curry with Mixed Leaves

SERVES 4

2 tablespoons peanut oil
  or vegetable oil

2 onions, thinly sliced

bunch of fine asparagus spears

14-ounce can coconut milk

2 tablespoons Thai red curry paste

3 fresh kaffir lime leaves

8 ounces baby spinach leaves,
  trimmed

2 heads bok choy, chopped

1 small head napa cabbage, shredded

handful of fresh cilantro, chopped

cooked rice, to serve

Method

1 Heat a wok over medium–high heat, then add the oil. Add the onions and asparagus and stir-fry for 1–2 minutes.

2 Add the coconut milk, curry paste, and lime leaves and bring gently to a boil, stirring occasionally. Add the spinach, bok choy, and cabbage and cook, stirring, for 2–3 minutes, until wilted. Add the cilantro and stir well. Serve immediately with rice.

84

Mixed Vegetables with Basil

2 tablespoons peanut oil or vegetable oil, plus extra for shallow frying

2 garlic cloves, chopped

1 onion, sliced

8 ears of baby corn, halved diagonally

1/2 cucumber, peeled, halved, seeded, and sliced

8-ounce can water chestnuts, drained and rinsed

1 cup snow peas

4 ounces shiitake mushrooms, halved

1 red bell pepper, seeded and thinly sliced

1 tablespoon light brown sugar

2 tablespoons Thai soy sauce

1 tablespoon Thai fish sauce

1 tablespoon rice vinegar

8-12 sprigs fresh Thai basil

freshly cooked, plain rice, to serve

Method

1 Heat a wok over high heat, then add the oil. Add the garlic and onion and stir-fry for 1–2 minutes. Add the baby corn, cucumber, water chestnuts, snow peas, mushrooms, and red bell pepper and stir-fry for 2–3 minutes, until starting to soften.

2 Add the sugar, soy sauce, fish sauce, and vinegar and gradually bring to a boil. Simmer for 1–2 minutes.

3 Meanwhile, heat enough oil for shallow-frying in a wok and, when hot, add the basil sprigs. Cook for 20–30 seconds, until crisp. Remove with a slotted spoon and drain on paper towels.

4 Garnish the vegetable stir-fry with the crispy basil and serve immediately with rice.

85

Hot & Sour Zucchini

SERVES 4

2 large zucchini, thinly sliced

1 teaspoon salt

2 tablespoons peanut oil

1 teaspoon Sichuan pepper, crushed

1/2 – 1 red chile, seeded and sliced
   into thin strips

1 large garlic clove, thinly sliced

1/2 teaspoon finely chopped
   fresh ginger

1 tablespoon rice vinegar

1 tablespoon light soy sauce

2 teaspoons sugar

1 scallion, green part included,
   thinly sliced

a few drops of sesame oil and
   1 teaspoon sesame seeds,
   to garnish

Method

1 Put the zucchini slices in a large colander and toss with the salt. Cover with a plate and put a weight on top. Let drain for 20 minutes. Rinse off the salt and spread out the slices on paper towels to dry.

2 Heat a wok over high heat and add the peanut oil. Add the Sichuan pepper, chile, garlic, and ginger. Heat for about 20 seconds, until the garlic is just beginning to color.

3 Add the zucchini slices and toss in the oil. Add the rice vinegar, soy sauce, and sugar and stir-fry for 2 minutes. Add the scallion and cook for 30 seconds. Sprinkle with the sesame oil and seeds, and serve immediately.

86

Eggplant Stir-Fry

SERVES 4

2 eggplants, peeled

1/3 cup plus 1 tablespoon peanut oil
 or vegetable oil

2 red bell peppers, seeded
 and cut into thin strips

1 cup canned water chestnuts,
 drained and sliced

6 scallions, sliced

2 teaspoons finely chopped
 fresh ginger

1 large garlic clove, thinly sliced

1 fresh green chile, seeded and
 finely chopped

2/3 cup hot vegetable stock

sesame seeds and thinly sliced
 scallions, to garnish

Sauce

1 1/2 tablespoons soy sauce

1 1/2 tablespoons rice vinegar

2 teaspoons sugar

2 teaspoons cornstarch, blended to a
 smooth paste with a little water

Method

1 For the sauce, combine the soy sauce, vinegar, and sugar in a small bowl, stirring to dissolve the sugar. Mix in the cornstarch paste and stir until smooth.

2 Slice the eggplants in half lengthwise. With the flat side facing down, slice each half lengthwise into 1/2-inch strips. Slice the wider strips lengthwise in half again, then cut all the strips widthwise into 1 1/2-inch pieces.

3 Heat a wok over high heat, then add 1/3 cup of the oil. Add the eggplant and red bell peppers and stir-fry for 2–3 minutes, until just beginning to color. Remove from the wok and drain on paper towels.

4 Heat the remaining tablespoon of oil in the wok over high heat. Stir-fry the water chestnuts, scallions, ginger, garlic, and chile for 1 minute.

5 Return the eggplant and red bell pepper to the wok. Reduce the heat to medium and add the sauce and stock. Stir-fry for 2–3 minutes, until slightly thickened. Sprinkle with sesame seeds and scallions and serve immediately.

87

Stir-Fried Butternut Squash

SERVES 2

1/2 butternut squash

6 large shiitake mushrooms

1/3 cup canola oil

1/2 teaspoon white peppercorns, crushed

1/2 teaspoon coriander seeds, crushed

sea salt flakes

2 large garlic cloves, thinly sliced

finely grated zest of 1/2 lemon

1/2 tablespoons rice vinegar

1/4 cup chicken stock or vegetable stock

2 good handfuls of baby spinach, trimmed

chopped fresh cilantro, to garnish

Method

1 Cut the squash in two between the neck and the rounded part. Remove the skin from each piece. Quarter the rounded section and remove the seeds and fibers. Slice lengthwise into thin segments. Slice the neck in half lengthwise, then widthwise into thin semicircles.

2 Remove and discard the tough stems from the mushrooms, and thinly slice the caps.

3 Heat a wok over medium–high heat, then add the oil. Add half of the crushed peppercorns and coriander seeds. Stir for a few seconds, then add the squash in small batches. Cook for 5–7 minutes, carefully turning with tongs, until lightly browned and just tender. Sprinkle with sea salt flakes. Using a slotted spoon, transfer to a large strainer set over a bowl.

4 Add the mushrooms to the wok and cook for 4–5 minutes, using some of the oil drained from the squash. Add the garlic and lemon zest, and cook for another minute. Sprinkle with sea salt flakes and the rest of the coriander seeds and peppercorns. Add to the squash.

5 Pour any oil drained from the vegetables into the wok. Stir in the vinegar and stock and simmer for a few seconds until slightly reduced.

6 Arrange the spinach on individual serving plates. Pile the vegetables on top, then pour over the juices from the wok. Sprinkle with cilantro and serve at once.

88

Mushrooms & Green Beans

SERVES 2

1 pound mixed small mushrooms
    such as cremini, enokim and
    buna shimeji

1/3 cup canola oil

1 teaspoon coriander seeds, crushed

1 fresh bay leaf

1 1/2 cups green beans

1 large garlic clove, thinly sliced

3 tablespoons lemon juice

2 teaspoons soy sauce

2 tablespoons chopped cilantro

2 teaspoons sesame oil

2 teaspoons sesame seeds

salt and pepper

Method

1 Rinse the mushrooms and dry with paper towels. If using clumping mushrooms, such as enoki and buna shimeji, slice off the root and separate the clump. Slice cremini mushrooms in half.

2 Heat a wok over medium–high heat and add the oil. Add the coriander seeds and bay leaf, and heat for a few seconds to flavor the oil. Add the mushrooms and beans and stir-fry for 5 minutes.

3 Stir in the garlic, lemon juice, and soy sauce. Season with salt and pepper and stir-fry for 2 minutes. Sprinkle with the cilantro, sesame oil, and seeds, and heat for a few seconds. Serve hot, warm, or at room temperature.

89

Oyster Mushrooms & Vegetable

SERVES 4

1 tablespoon peanut oil
   or vegetable oil

4 scallions, finely sliced

1 carrot, cut into thin strips

1 zucchini, cut into thin strips

1/2 head broccoli, cut into florets

1 pound oyster mushrooms,
   thinly sliced

2 tablespoons chunky peanut butter

1 teaspoon chili powder, or to taste

3 tablespoons water

lime wedges, to garnish

freshly cooked rice, to serve

Method

1 Heat the oil in a preheated wok or large skillet until almost smoking. Stir-fry the scallions for 1 minute. Add the carrot and zucchini and stir-fry for another minute. Then add the broccoli and cook for an additional 1 minute.

2 Stir in the mushrooms and cook until they are soft and at least half of the liquid they produce has evaporated. Add the peanut butter and stir well, then season with the chili powder. Finally, add the water and cook for 1 minute.

3 Garnish with lime wedges and serve with freshly cooked rice.

90

Vegetable Stir-Fry

SERVES 4

2 tablespoons peanut oil or
   vegetable oil

1 bunch of scallions,
   coarsely chopped

1-inch piece fresh ginger,
   finely chopped

2 lemongrass stalks, halved

2 carrots, cut into matchsticks

1 small head broccoli,
   cut into florets

4 ears of baby corn, halved
   lengthwise

1/2 cup of canned water chestnuts,
   drained

1 tablespoon red curry paste

8 ounces dried medium
   egg noodles

1/4 cup sesame seeds

salt

Method

1 Heat the oil in a preheated wok, add the scallions, ginger, and lemongrass, and stir-fry over medium–high heat for 2–3 minutes, until starting to soften. Add the carrots, broccoli, and baby corn and stir-fry for 3–4 minutes, until starting to soften. Add the water chestnuts and curry paste and stir well, then stir-fry for another 2–3 minutes. Discard the lemongrass.

2 Meanwhile, bring a large saucepan of lightly salted water to a boil, add the noodles, and cook for 4–5 minutes, or according to the package directions, until just tender. Drain and return to the saucepan. Add the sesame seeds and toss to coat.

3 Add the noodles to the stir-fried vegetables and serve immediately.

91

Carrot & Pumpkin Curry

SERVES 4

2/3 cup vegetable stock

1-inch piece fresh galangal or ginger, sliced

2 garlic cloves, chopped

1 lemongrass stalk (white part only), finely chopped

2 fresh red chiles, seeded and chopped

4 carrots, cut into chunks

2 cups peeled, seeded, and cubed pumpkin or butternut squash

2 tablespoons peanut oil or vegetable oil

2 shallots, finely chopped

3 tablespoons Thai yellow curry paste

14-ounce can coconut milk

4–6 sprigs of fresh Thai basil

2 tablespoons toasted pumpkin seeds, to garnish

Method

1 Pour the stock into a large saucepan and bring to a boil. Add the galangal, half of the garlic, the lemongrass, and chiles and simmer for 5 minutes. Add the carrots and pumpkin and simmer for 5–6 minutes, until tender.

2 Meanwhile, heat the oil in a wok or skillet and stir-fry the shallots and the remaining garlic for 2–3 minutes. Add the curry paste and stir-fry for 1–2 minutes.

3 Stir the shallot mixture into the saucepan and add the coconut milk and Thai basil. Simmer for 2–3 minutes. Serve hot, sprinkled with the toasted pumpkin seeds.

92

Tofu & Vegetable Curry

SERVES 4

peanut oil or vegetable oil,
  for deep-frying

1 1/2 cups firm tofu cubes

2 tablespoons peanut oil or
  vegetable oil

2 onions, chopped

2 garlic cloves, chopped

1 fresh red chile, seeded and sliced

3 celery stalks, diagonally sliced

3 cups thickly sliced white button
  mushrooms

8 ears of baby corn, cut in half

1 red bell pepper, seeded and
  cut into strips

3 tablespoons Thai red curry paste

14-ounce can coconut milk

1 teaspoon palm sugar or light
  brown sugar

2 tablespoons Thai soy sauce

8 ounces baby spinach leaves

Method

1 Heat the oil for deep-frying in a preheated wok or a deep saucepan to 350–375°F, or until a cube of bread browns in 30 seconds. Add the tofu cubes, in batches, and cook for 4–5 minutes, until crisp and brown all over. Remove with a slotted spoon and drain on paper towels.

2 Heat the 2 tablespoons of oil in a wok or skillet and stir-fry the onions, garlic, and chile for 1–2 minutes, until they start to soften. Add the celery, mushrooms, baby corn, and red bell pepper and stir-fry for 3–4 minutes, until they soften.

3 Stir in the curry paste and coconut milk and gradually bring to a boil. Add the sugar and soy sauce and then the spinach. Cook, stirring continuously, until the spinach has wilted. Serve immediately, topped with the tofu.

93

Snow Peas & Tofu Stir-Fry

SERVES 2–3

2 tablespoons sesame oil

3 tablespoons peanut oil

7 ounces small shiitake mushrooms

2 heads bok choy, leaves left whole, stems sliced

2½ cups snow peas, diagonally halved

1½ cups firm tofu cubes

1¼-inch piece fresh ginger, thinly sliced

2 garlic cloves, finely chopped

1 tablespoon soy sauce

1 teaspoon sesame seeds

salt and pepper

cooked noodles, to serve

Method

1 Heat a wok with a lid over medium–high heat, then add the oils. Add the mushrooms, bok choy stems, and snow peas, and stir-fry for 1 minute.

2 Add the tofu, bok choy leaves, ginger, garlic, and a splash of water to moisten. Stir-fry for another 1–2 minutes, until the bok choy leaves have wilted.

3 Stir in the soy sauce, sprinkle with the sesame seeds, and season with salt and pepper. Serve immediately with noodles.

94

Spicy Tofu

SERVES 4

1 1/2 cups firm tofu cubes

4 tablespoons peanut oil
 or vegetable oil

1 tablespoon grated fresh ginger

3 garlic cloves, crushed

4 scallions, thinly sliced

1 head broccoli, cut into florets

1 carrot, cut into thin strips

1 yellow bell pepper, seeded
 and thinly sliced

9 ounces shiitake mushrooms,
 thinly sliced

steamed rice, to serve

Marinade

1/3 cup vegetable stock

2 teaspoons cornstarch

2 tablespoons soy sauce

1 tablespoon sugar

pinch of crushed red pepper

Method

1 To make the marinade, blend the vegetable stock, cornstarch, soy sauce, sugar, and crushed red pepper together in a large bowl. Add the tofu and toss well to cover in the marinade. Set aside to marinate for 20 minutes.

2 In a large wok, heat 2 tablespoons of the peanut oil and stir-fry the tofu with its marinade until brown and crispy. Remove from the wok and set aside.

3 Heat the remaining 2 tablespoons of peanut oil in the wok and stir-fry the ginger, garlic, and scallions for 30 seconds. Add the broccoli, carrot, yellow bell pepper, and mushrooms to the wok and cook for 5–6 minutes. Return the tofu to the wok and stir-fry to reheat. Serve immediately over freshly steamed rice.

95

Tofu Laksa with Noodles

SERVES 4

3 1/2 cups vegetable stock

14-ounce can coconut milk

9 ounces shiitake mushrooms, stems removed, thinly sliced

1 cup firm tofu cubes

2 tablespoons tomato paste

6 ounces fine egg noodles

salt and pepper

8 scallions, sliced, and 1/4 cup shredded mint leaves, to garnish

lime wedges, to serve

Spice paste

2 red chiles, seeded and chopped

1 1/2-inch piece fresh ginger, chopped

2 large garlic cloves, chopped

2 lemongrass stalks, tough outer layers removed, inner stalks chopped

1 teaspoon coriander seeds, crushed

6 macadamia nuts, chopped

small handful of cilantro leaves

3 tablespoons vegetable oil

Method

1 Puree the spice paste ingredients in a food processor, pulsing several times until smooth.

2 Heat a wok over medium–high heat, add the spice paste, and stir-fry for 30 seconds. Pour in the stock and coconut milk, and bring to a boil. Add the mushrooms, tofu, and tomato paste and season with salt and pepper. Simmer gently for 5 minutes.

3 Bring a large saucepan of lightly salted water to a boil, add the noodles, and cook for 4 minutes, or according to the package directions, until soft. Divide among four large, warm soup bowls. Ladle the spicy broth over the noodles. Garnish with sliced scallions and shredded mint leaves and serve with lime wedges.

96

Crispy Noodle Stir-Fry

SERVES 4

peanut oil or sunflower oil,
   for deep-frying

4 ounces rice vermicelli, broken
   into 3-inch lengths

1 cup green beans, cut into
   short lengths

2 carrots, cut into thin sticks

2 zucchini, cut into thin sticks

4 ounces shiitake mushrooms, sliced

1-inch piece fresh ginger, shredded

1/2 small head napa cabbage,
   shredded

4 scallions, shredded

1 cup fresh bean sprouts

2 tablespoons dark soy sauce

2 tablespoons Chinese rice wine
   or dry sherry

large pinch of sugar

2 tablespoons coarsely chopped
   fresh cilantro

Method

1 Heat a large wok over high heat. Pour in the oil and heat to 350-375°F, or until a cube of bread browns in 30 seconds. Add the noodles, in batches, and cook for 1 1/2–2 minutes, or until crisp and puffed up. Remove and drain on paper towels. Pour off all but 2 tablespoons of oil from the wok.

2 Heat the remaining oil over high heat. Add the green beans and stir-fry for 2 minutes. Add the carrot and zucchini sticks, sliced mushrooms, and ginger and stir-fry for another 2 minutes.

3 Add the shredded napa cabbage, scallions, and bean sprouts and stir-fry for another minute. Add the soy sauce, rice wine, and sugar and cook, stirring continuously, for 1 minute.

4 Add the chopped cilantro and toss well. Serve immediately, with the noodles.

97

Noodles with Tofu & Mushrooms

SERVES 4

3 tablespoons peanut oil
  or vegetable oil

2 dried red chiles

8 ounces medium egg noodles

1 garlic clove, crushed

1 1/4 cups firm tofu cubes

8 ounces oyster or cremini
  mushrooms, sliced

2 tablespoons lime juice

2 tablespoons soy sauce

1 teaspoon brown sugar

fresh red chiles, to garnish

Method

1 Heat the oil in a wok and add the chiles. Heat gently for 10 minutes. Discard the fried chiles.

2 Cook the noodles in boiling water for 4 minutes, or according to the package directions, until tender. Drain.

3 Add the garlic and tofu to the wok and stir-fry on high heat until golden. Remove with a slotted spoon and keep hot.

4 Add the mushrooms to the wok and stir-fry for 2–3 minutes, until soften.

5 Stir in the lime juice, soy sauce, and sugar.

6 Return the noodles and tofu to the wok and toss to mix thoroughly.

7 Serve immediately, garnished with fresh chiles.

98

Noodle Stir-Fry

SERVES 2

5 ounces dried wide rice noodles

1/3 cup soy sauce

2 tablespoons lemon juice

1 teaspoon sugar

1/2 teaspoon cornstarch

1 tablespoon peanut oil
  or vegetable oil

2 teaspoons grated fresh ginger

2 garlic cloves, chopped

4–5 scallions, sliced

2 tablespoons Chinese rice wine
  or dry sherry

8-ounce can water chestnuts,
  drained and sliced

Method

1 Put the noodles in a large bowl, cover with boiling water, and soak for 4 minutes, or cook according to the package directions, until tender. Drain and rinse under cold running water.

2 Combine the soy sauce, lemon juice, sugar, and cornstarch in a small bowl.

3 Heat a wok over medium–high heat, then add the oil. Add the ginger, and garlic and stir-fry for 1 minute. Add the scallions and stir-fry for 3 minutes.

4 Add the rice wine, then the soy sauce mixture and cook for 1 minute.

5 Stir in the water chestnuts and noodles and cook for another 1–2 minutes, or until heated through. Serve immediately.

99

Egg-Fried Rice

SERVES 4

2 tablespoons peanut oil or
   vegetable oil

2 1/2 cups chilled cooked rice

1 egg, well beaten

Method

1 Heat the oil in a preheated wok and stir-fry the rice
for 1 minute, breaking it down as much as possible into
individual grains.

2 Quickly add the egg, stirring, coating each grain of rice.
Stir until the egg is cooked and the rice, as much as possible, is
separated into single grains. Serve immediately.

100

Spring Vegetable Rice

SERVES 4

2 tablespoons peanut oil
  or vegetable oil

2 shallots, chopped

2 garlic cloves, crushed

1¼ cups long-grain rice

about 2½ cups chicken stock

1 tablespoon Thai red curry paste

1 teaspoon Thai fish sauce

3 tablespoons soy sauce

12 ears of baby corn,
  halved lengthwise

12 baby carrots, halved lengthwise

1 cup sugar snap peas

½ cup fresh bean sprouts

¼ cup sesame seeds

handful of fresh cilantro, chopped

2 tablespoons sesame oil

salt

Method

1 Heat a wok over medium–high heat, then add the peanut oil. Add the shallots and garlic and stir-fry for 1–2 minutes. Add the rice and stir-fry for 2–3 minutes.

2 Add the stock, curry paste, fish sauce, and soy sauce and bring to a boil, stirring occasionally. Reduce the heat and simmer for 10–12 minutes, until the rice is tender, adding more stock or boiling water, if necessary.

3 Meanwhile, cook the baby corn and carrots in a saucepan of lightly salted boiling water for 2–3 minutes, until just tender. Add the sugar snap peas and cook for 1 minute. Add the bean sprouts and stir well, then drain.

4 Heat a dry skillet until hot, add the sesame seeds, and cook over medium–high heat, shaking the skillet frequently, for 30–45 seconds, until lightly browned.

5 Add the drained vegetables, cilantro, and sesame oil to the rice and mix well. Serve immediately, scattered with the toasted sesame seeds.

Index

Thai-Style Seafood Soup 38

seafood
  Quick Seafood Rice 162
  Seafood Chow Mein 158
  Seafood Curry 160
  Thai-Style Seafood Soup 38

sesame
  Crispy Sesame Shrimp 20
  Hot Sesame Beef 64
  Sesame Noodles with Shrimp 168

shallots
  Beef & Bok Choy Stir-Fry 70
  Beef & Noodle Soup 28
  Beef with Mixed Mushrooms 72
  Carrot & Pumpkin Curry 198
  Chicken Fried Rice 118
  Pad Noodles with Pork & Shrimp 90

shrimp
  Crispy Sesame Shrimp 20
  Egg Rolls 10
  Pad Noodles with Pork & Shrimp 90
  Seafood Chow Mein 158
  Seafood Curry 160
  Sesame Noodles with Shrimp 168
  Shrimp Fu Yung 150
  Shrimp Noodle Bowl 166
  Shrimp Toasts 18
  Spicy Crab & Shrimp Salad 50
  Squid & Shrimp Laksa 34
  Teriyaki Shrimp 164
  Thai-Style Seafood Soup 38
  Yaki Soba 106
Sichuan Peppered Beef 60
Sliced Beef in Black Bean Sauce 56

snow peas
  Ginger Beef with Yellow Peppers 68
  Gingered Chicken Salad 46
  Hot & Sour Vegetable Salad 48
  Snow Peas & Tofu Stir-Fry 202
  Marinated Beef with Vegetables 66
  Peppered Chicken Stir-Fry 108
  Scallop & Snow Peas Stir-Fry 172

Spicy Crab & Shrimp Salad 50
Three-Pea Stir-Fry with Duck 136
Spice Chicken with Zucchini 116
Spicy Crab & Shrimp Salad 50
Spicy Tofu 204

spinach
  Chinese Rice with Egg 16
  Lemon Turkey with Spinach 128
  Marinated Beef with Vegetables 66
  Red Curry with Mixed Leaves 182
Spring Vegetable Rice 216

squid
  Seafood Chow Mein 158
  Seafood Curry 160
  Squid & Shrimp Laksa 34
  Squid with Black Bean Sauce 178
Steamed Salmon with Asparagus 152
Stir-Fried Butternut Squash 190
Stir-Fried Crab with Ginger 174
Stir-Fried Lamb with Orange 78
Stir-Fried Salmon with Leeks 154
Sweet & Sour Chicken 104
Sweet & Sour Pork 84
Sweet & Sour Spareribs 30

Tempura Vegetables 24
Teriyaki Chicken 110
Teriyaki Shrimp 164
Teriyaki Tuna with Vegetables 156
Teriyaki Turkey 122
Thai Green Fish Curry 140
Thai-Style Seafood Soup 38
Three-Pea Stir-Fry with Duck 136

tofu
  Gado Gado 52
  Hot & Sour Soup Tom Yum 36
  Snow Peas & Tofu Stir-Fry 202
  Spicy Tofu 204
  Tofu & Vegetable Curry 200
  Tofu Laksa with Noodles 206

tomatoes
  Duck with Mixed Bell Peppers 130

Fish with Tomatoes & Herbs 148
Quick Seafood Rice 162

tuna
  Teriyaki Tuna with Vegetables 156

turkey
  Lemon Turkey with Spinach 128
  Turkey Teriyaki 122
  Turkey with Bok Choy 124
  Turkey with Hoisin Sauce 126

vegetables
  Hot & Sour Vegetable Salad 48
  Marinated Beef with Vegetables 66
  Mixed Vegetables with Basil 184
  Oyster Mushrooms & Vegetables 194
  Spring Vegetable Rice 216
  Tempura Vegetables 24
  Teriyaki Tuna with Vegetables 156
  Tofu & Vegetable Curry 200
  Vegetable Stir-Fry 196

water chestnuts
  Beef Chop Suey 62
  Chicken with Pistachio Nuts 114
  Eggplant Stir-Fry 188
  Noodle Stir-Fry 212
  Peppered Chicken Stir-Fry 108
  Pork with Basil & Lemongrass 88
  Red Lamb Curry 82
  Vegetable Stir-Fry 196

wontons
  Crab Wontons 22
  Crispy Pork Dumplings 12
  Pork & Cabbage Gyoza 14

Yaki Soba 106

zucchini
  Hot & Sour Zucchini 186
  Oyster Mushrooms & Vegetables 194
  Pork with Basil & Lemongrass 88
  Spice Chicken with Zucchini 116